Parenting Against The Current

Taking Back Discipleship in Your Home

by
JOSHUA POTEET
and
MATT NATIONS

Copyright © 2025 Josh Poteet and Matt Nations. All rights reserved.

No part of this publication may be reproduced, stored in a retrieval system, or transmitted in any form or by any means—electronic, mechanical, photocopying, recording, or otherwise—without the prior written permission of the authors.

First Edition

Cover design by **Saulo Jonatan**
Published by **Growmentum Press**
This imprint is used for branding purposes only. Rights are retained by the authors.

Scripture quotations are taken from the **Holy Bible, New International Version®, NIV®**. Copyright © 1973, 1978, 1984, 2011 by Biblica, Inc.®

This is a work of nonfiction. Real names, stories, and experiences are used with permission or altered for clarity and privacy.

ISBN
979-8-9986392-0-3

Printed in the United States of America

Parenting Against The Current

Taking Back Discipleship in Your Home

Endorsements

Parenting Against the Current is written by a practitioner in disciple-making. There are plenty of books on parenting; however, Josh and Matt do a great job—using humor and practical advice—of giving us, as parents, a guidebook on how to disciple our kids.
Bob Reed, Lead Pastor of CyLife Church

If you want to grow in your parenting and connection with your kids in today's world, you need to read this book. Every parent will benefit and be inspired by Josh and Matt's contribution to the Christian community through their stories and perspective in *Parenting Against the Current*.
Brandon Guindon, Senior Pastor of Real Life Ministries Texas.

Parenting Against the Current offers what today's parents desperately need: practical wisdom grounded in biblical truth. This is more than just another parenting book—it's a companion for the journey. Whether you're struggling with cultural pressures or simply seeking to disciple your children more effectively, this book will equip and encourage you. A must-read for parents committed to swimming against the current and raising children who thrive.
Chris Goeppner, Founding Pastor, Riverbank Church, Vermont/New Hampshire

Parenting Against the Current takes a fresh approach to a timely topic: the biblical responsibility of parents as the primary disciple-makers of their children. The church and trusted others certainly play a part, but as parents, we must understand our calling. It does well to draw our attention to this wonderful and weighty responsibility, offering helpful tips, questions, and challenges that make it practical. It's well worth your time to read—and implement.
Tim Ponzani, Executive Vice President of Converge

Parenting Against the Current is deeply rooted in Scripture, full of humility, and refreshingly honest. It doesn't heap on guilt; it offers hope, clarity, and a path forward. This book reads like a conversation with a trusted mentor. It's funny, deeply personal, and calls you to something greater without being overwhelming. I'll be recommending it often.
Dawn Marraccino, Executive & Life Coach | Ministry Consultant

To my great loves,

To Jennie, for being my teammate through all seasons. To Lilla, for being the goof that I can laugh with over nothing at all. And to the Ez-man for being my in-home wrestling partner (someday, you'll be able to take me). You each have my heart and inspire me to lean ever more on Jesus as I grow as a disciple, husband, and father.

~ Josh

To Kai, Jayse, River, and Shiloh—

You are such gifts and my most important disciples. My prayer is that you grow to love Jesus deeply, follow Him wholeheartedly, and live as sons and a daughter of the King. May your lives be marked by faith, courage, and a passion for His glory. May our home always be a place of grace, truth, and kingdom purpose.

~ Matt

Table of Contents

INTRODUCTION: THE CURRENT — 7

PART 1: YOU, THEM, AND US — 13

CHAPTER 1: Kids Were Made for Strawberries — 15

CHAPTER 2: Zooming In — 35

CHAPTER 3: A Connection Issue — 53

CHAPTER 4: Family Trip — 79

CHAPTER 5: It Takes a Village to Raise A Parent — 107

PART 2: WHAT'S NEXT — 129

CHAPTER 6: Fail Forward — 131

CHAPTER 7: Intentional Answers — 153

CHAPTER 8: Control or Direct — 177

CHAPTER 9: Needs Based Parenting — 203

CHAPTER 10: Own It — 223

Resources — 231
Acknowledgments — 235
About the Authors — 237
Thank You for Reading! — 245
Stay in Touch — 246

The Current

Whirlpools are intense. No, I'm not talking about your casual bathroom jacuzzi. Picture a Captain Jack Sparrow kind of whirlpool where someone swam to the sea floor and pulled the plug. Tranquil waters suddenly transform into a swirling vortex, threatening to pull in anyone who isn't paying attention or showing it the respect it demands. That, my friend, is what parenting feels like. No, I'm not saying your kids are conspiring to drown you, but that life itself has a current eager to drag you under.

As a parent, you've probably already felt this pull. It's that relentless force tugging you away from intentional parenting and into something else entirely. Let's be clear—this isn't just a metaphor taken too far. The "current" is anything that stops you from being the intentional parent God has created you to be. Exhaustion? That's the current. Mismanaging your schedule or finances? That's part of it, too. Add in personal sin, overhyped desires, distance from God, and a lack of community, and you've got a whirlpool powerful enough to shipwreck your family. This current represents the culture of the world, which means that if we aren't intentionally moving against it, we'll be taken by it.

I'm not saying this is your goal. You're reading this book because you want the best for your family. You want them to grow, thrive, and experience the fruit of your parenting efforts. But here's the truth: it's going to take work. All it takes to get pulled deeper into the current is a lack of focus. Think about it. When you're at the beach, playing in the water, you might not notice the current tugging at you. Then, thirty minutes later, you look up to find your beach umbrella, cooler, and My Little Pony beach towel a quarter mile down the shore. Only then do you realize—it wasn't your stuff that moved; it was you. Drift is subtle, often so gradual that you don't even notice it unless you're paying attention.

Have you ever looked around and asked yourself, "How did we end up here?" Are you fighting against the current, or has it swept you away? Are your kids jumping into life rafts, eager to chart their own course? Do you feel alone, tired, or burnt out? Here's the good news: it's less about where you are right now and more about where you're going. Every parent experiences drift. The key is recognizing it, turning the ship around, and moving toward something better. And here's my promise to you: parenting against the current will be exhausting. At times, it will feel defeating. But it will also be one of the most rewarding things you will ever do.

My wife, Jennie, and I have a five-year-old daughter named Lilla, and we have another one on the way. It's up to us to seize every opportunity to help our kids know Jesus. We can't accept Jesus on their behalf—that's their decision. However, intentional parenting is about pointing our children toward Jesus and showing them our journey with Him in tangible and, hopefully, contagious ways. We can't save them—that's God's role—but you'd better believe we're doing everything we can to make the introduction as they begin their own walk with their Creator.

That all sounds great, but the truth is, we're still learning how to read the map while trying to row in the right direction, just like everyone else. By the time you become a veteran parent, your kids are no longer living under your roof. I can't pretend to have all the answers or to hold the secret sauce (which I'm pretty sure Chick-fil-A has a patent on anyway) that solves everyone's parenting challenges. Like I said, I'm figuring this out just like the next parent. What I can offer is a collection of experiences with other parents, a treasure trove of stories born out of my own mistakes, and an unshakable trust that Jesus can use these words for His good.

Disclaimer: I recognize that our family dynamics, marital situations, and the makeup of our children may be vastly different. God's creativity ensured that He didn't use a cookie-cutter approach in creation—especially when it comes to our children. Each one is beautifully unique, with specific needs, weaknesses, and strengths. As parents, we are the primary disciple-makers of our kids. Our role is to shepherd their hearts closer to Jesus.

In short, this book is designed to share helpful strategies and lessons we've learned from our mistakes as we work to intentionally lead our family and others.

Will it be easy? No. Moving against the current never is. But it's time to pick up our oars and start rowing in a new direction. This is a battle cry for parental warriors who are ready to intentionally train, equip, and send out giant slayers. It's for parents who want to get off the bench and step onto the field. It's for those determined to reject the passivity of being dragged under and start moving against the current toward a new destination.

It will be sacrificial because parenting is sacrificial. When in doubt, look to the cross. There is a cost in parenting, just as there is a cost in love. I'm not telling you anything you don't already know, but sometimes we all need the reminder: parenting is always about moving against the current.

Think about it. What does a current do other than pull you away from where you're meant to be? Ships aren't designed to sit on the ocean floor; they're made to carry precious cargo, soaring across the waves toward their destination. And that's precisely the problem: we often don't realize we're being pulled under because we haven't clearly defined where we're supposed to be or where we're headed.

Intentional parenting isn't the destination. It's the vessel. We don't fight the current just for the sake of fighting. Exhaustion isn't the goal (though it's often a byproduct). So, where are you parenting your kids toward?

For many of us, the issue is a lack of a clearly defined destination. How do you know if you're winning in your parenting? How do you know if you're hitting the mark or drifting away from it? What milestones should you anticipate along the way? How do you inspect your trajectory to escape the whirlpool and get back on course?

Twenty years from now, what do you want the result of your parenting to be?

We need to understand the intended destination of our parenting. And I challenge you to let that destination be guided by Scripture, not worldly wisdom. Destinations rooted in the world are like foundations built on sand; they crumble just as easily. For that reason, your child's success, as defined by the world, cannot be the ultimate target. Achieving a "good" job, living a "good" life, or simply being a "good" person are all short-sighted goals that prioritize the here and now at the expense of eternity.

A few years ago, I heard a pastor share the two main targets he and his wife had for their parenting. They wanted their kids to deeply love Jesus (Proverbs 22:6) and for their kids to desire to be with them even when they didn't have to be (Proverbs 17:6). I loved this perspective and adopted it for our home. Everything we do as a family is viewed through the lens of growing our love for God and strengthening our fellowship with each other.

I want our children to have a desire to grow with God that isn't dependent on us as their parents. And that's not easy. As a Student Pastor, I see kids come in carrying their parents' faith like a backpack. They show up for their parents. They pray for their parents. They serve for their parents. Honestly, that's not a bad thing. It's actually a great start. In fact, that's how it's designed to begin. But their faith must become their own for it to sustain them long-term.

Your faith (or lack of faith) directly impacts your family, which is why I want a relationship with God that makes my family jealous for Jesus. I don't mean a sinful jealousy that feeds my pride. I want my relationship with Jesus to be so visible, so genuine, that it creates a deep longing within my family to pursue their own personal relationship with Him.

Your children may carry your faith for a season, but eventually, it has to become their own.

Today, while driving our daughter to school, she told me she had Jesus in her heart. I smiled and asked her what that meant, and she needed help talking through it. She had heard Jennie and me share our love for Jesus and wanted a relationship with Him, too. Here's the problem: at five years old, I could convince my daughter that I had discovered a magical Cheeto that gave me super strength and sweet cheese powers. Obviously, I wouldn't do that (probably), but she'd believe me because she trusts me. Our kids often begin stepping toward a relationship with Jesus because of their relationship with their parents, and the relationship they see their parents have with God. That's wonderful. But as we disciple our kids, we need to remember that our faith was never meant to save or sustain them. It can't. They need their own. It's through the everyday, daily grind that our children begin to realize their need to independently walk with Jesus.

At some point, they will have their own ship, and the current will pull at them just as it pulls at you. Proverbs 22:6 says, *"Train up a child in the way he should go; even when he is old, he will not depart from it."* We are training our kids to sink or swim, to be pulled under, or to strive toward a greater destination. If we do our part now, we are better preparing and empowering our kids for the day they steer their own boats!

It's about raising godly men and women who are deeply in love with Jesus. It's about them hearing His heartbeat and dancing to the rhythm it creates. If you're not yet a disciple of Christ, I'm grateful you've made it this far, and I encourage you to keep going. My prayer is that you'll find many practical parenting tools here. But even more, I hope to share my life and the transformative impact Jesus has had on me. He is the only hope we have of being the parents He created us to be. If you are a believer, I hope this book serves as a strategic and practical reminder of our need to tether ourselves to Jesus as we continue moving upstream.

The most important destination our children can reach is a deep love for Christ. This is the target this book is navigating toward. Every page and chapter is designed to offer pieces of a map that will help you move against the current toward safe harbor. You are in the captain's chair. As you sail these waters, take in the views, steer clear of the whirlpool, and enjoy the journey. It's a beautiful scene, made even sweeter by those onboard with you.

Part 1:
You, Them, and Us

Kids Were Made for Strawberries

There's a story pastors tell about a father who took his son through a strawberry patch. As they walked, the father picked a strawberry off the vine and took a bite. Afterward, he handed his son another strawberry, which was just as good. It was wonderful. Every bite was filled with perfect flavor that they both enjoyed together. But as time passed, things changed. People, as they often do, began to treat the strawberries differently. They stopped picking and enjoying them fresh. Instead, the strawberries were chopped up into little pieces and used in things like fruit salads and cakes.

It got to the point where the whole strawberry wasn't necessary anymore. Instead, they had products made with strawberry extract or the essence of strawberry. They got things like strawberry Pop-Tarts and strawberry-flavored soda. Eventually, they reached a place where the strawberry itself was no longer needed. There was now a way to create strawberry flavor without ever using an actual strawberry. One day, the father gave his son a strawberry slush that didn't contain any real strawberries, and the boy loved it. Every day, his dad would give him the strawberry slush, and neither thought much about the strawberries or the field. Then, one day, the father and son walked again through the strawberry patch. The father reached over and picked a fresh strawberry for the boy to try. The boy took a bite, but didn't like the taste. It didn't taste like the strawberry slush he had grown to love.

This story is often used to explain how the Gospel is watered down, altered, and eventually becomes something entirely different. However, it also carries direct implications for our own walk with Jesus and our role as disciple-making parents. Ask someone nearby how their relationship with Jesus is going, and you'll likely hear that it's "pretty good." But what are they comparing "good" to? Often, we settle and compare our relationship with Jesus to something like a strawberry-flavored Pop-Tart, which we mistakenly call normal. It's "good" because we have a job, we pray at meals, and we go through the motions. But that's not what our relationship with Jesus was meant to be. This is a back-to-the-garden conversation, where the strawberries were picked straight off the vine, and God walked side by side with humans. That's the kind of relationship we are meant to pursue.

This drift has directly affected our parenting. We sacrifice intentionality for TV and our sabbaths for soccer games. I get it. I've been there. This isn't a judgment, but a conviction upon my heart as I recognize my own drift and my need to return to the design. Our kids were made for strawberries. They were made for the real thing. There have been times when I allowed the television to take up more real estate in my day than it should have and times when I wasn't as intentional as I should have been. And in the moments when I tried to steer my family back to the garden, our daughter didn't always like the taste. She preferred TV over curious questions about her heart. Returning to the garden isn't the easy path, but it's exactly where we need to head if we're going to be the parents we were created to be. We need to stop the drift and take a stand.

> **Our kids were made for strawberries. They were made for the real thing.**

We need to parent against the current. But here's the tough part: none of us entered the parenting game with a plan to abdicate our roles and drift from intentionality. It happened on its own, slowly, often without us even noticing.

As a kid, my family went to a waterpark for my dad's work every year. We loved the slides, the cannonball contests, eating ice cream from plastic buckets, and especially the lazy river. My brothers and I would play tag and often run against the current (yeah, we were those kids) as we tried to escape each other's grasp. As we worked against the current, we had to be careful, or the momentum of the stream would sweep us away. Not only that, but if we tried to stand still, we'd get hit by tubes or lose our focus and be pushed forward again.

We live in such a current. This world has a current that is pulling at every one of us. All it takes is a loss of focus, and we're pulled away from the intentional parenting we were meant to embrace. It's exhausting, and honestly, it would be easier if we could just sit in a tube and float down the river. Maybe that's what heaven will be like, where the current is shifted toward God, and everything flows in His direction. But that's not where we live today. If we're not intentional about discipling our kids, we will leave them—and ourselves—exposed to a current that intends to carry us away.

As parents, this can easily become our reality. We may have intentionally shared the Gospel with our children at the start; we may have worked hard to disciple them, but let's be honest, Poptarts are so much easier than finding a strawberry patch, and going with the flow requires less effort. As a result, our kids grow up not knowing the Gospel, not understanding what a relationship with Jesus can look like, and at best, they have poor imitations of the real thing. We get tired and trade crops for toasters. We stop talking about Jesus in our homes because it takes time, effort, and intentionality. Work takes all our energy, and we have nothing left. We allow our schedules to push Jesus out, and we forget to keep Him at the center of everything.

> **We get tired and trade crops for toasters.**

And just like that, we expect pastors and ministry leaders to disciple our kids because, frankly, we are too busy and feel ill-equipped. As a pastor, I love the kids I get to shepherd and lead. It's a gift to pour into these students each week, but I cannot disciple them all. I have nearly forty faithful volunteers who crush it in our ministry, and with their help, we still can't come close to discipling them all. And that's just in our church. Our kids don't need more student pastors. They need parents who are prayed up, armored up, and take their role as primary disciple-makers seriously.

Pause. If you're in ministry, I've seen this flipped around. It's easy to give everything that you have to the church while your family survives on your leftovers. After all, you're serving God! There are so many people in need! Too many church leaders have sacrificed their families on the altar of ministry. Don't get it twisted. Your primary ministry is your home. Don't be so focused on other ships that you forget to put life jackets on your kids. Don't let the current drag you away from the people who God entrusted you to love and lead. Okay, we're good. **Unpause.**

For some, this drift may not have started with your parenting but in your childhood. The model you have for raising kids may not have led you upstream, leaving you rowing without a map. Know that many of the most intentional parents started here. This could be the start of a wonderful change of direction. It's time to toss out the slush, grab the hands of those we love most, and head upriver toward the garden. There are strawberries there, and if you care, I'm pretty sure they're organic.

di-SKI-ple?

When my daughter was born, I read countless parenting books, practiced changing diapers, took a strange birthing class with my wife, and sought advice from all our friends with kids. Yet, when I held that little girl in my arms for the first time, I knew I was completely out of my depth. I asked, "How much sunlight does this thing need, and when do I water it?" As ready as I thought I was, I was wildly unprepared.

Obviously, I'm kidding…mostly, but I did have one big question. How do I disciple my daughter? This was something I had never experienced growing up. I didn't know how to do it, but I knew I needed to. This is the struggle of most Christ-loving parents. We know we want them to love the Lord, but we don't know what it looks like to walk beside them intentionally.

The first (and only time) I went skiing was in Germany. My unit in the Army had been sent to train at a small base in *Hohenfels* for a month. One morning, my Sergeant walked in and asked, "Who wants to go skiing in the Bavarian Alps this Friday?" I responded that I would, but unfortunately, I was on shift that day. He shrugged and said, "That's not what I asked." I was in! I couldn't have been more excited. I was about to go skiing for the first time, and it was in Germany! That Friday, I went to the ski shop, got everything the head ski teacher/master/salesmen/ninja/dude recommended, and jumped on the bus.

By the time we got to the slope, I was bursting with adrenaline. As I ran past a German couple, I quickly asked, "Where's the bunny slope?" Even at 23, I had the wisdom to keep it simple. They looked at me, a little confused, and pointed to a nearby lift. That's all I needed. As I took the lift, I found it odd that the bunny slopes were at the top of the mountain, but what do I know? I'm just a guy from Florida. Once I reached the top, I jumped off the lift without much thought and began my descent. As I started down the hill, a couple of thoughts crossed my mind. First, I'd seen professional skiers control their speed by zigging back and forth. I tried it. It worked! The second thought went something like this: "I must be the most athletic man in the world. Look at me go! I'm amazing! I've never done this before, and I'm tackling this mountain faster than anyone around me!" As I picked up speed and saw the bottom approaching, another thought popped into my mind, *I had absolutely no idea how to stop*!

I learned to water ski in Florida, but these two types of skiing presented very different challenges. In the aquatic version of the sport, the most challenging part to master was getting out of the water. Stopping had never been a problem…until now.

I looked to the bottom of the mountain, and things got worse. Instead of the 500-foot landing strip that I imagined must exist for a gradual stop, I saw a wall of two-foot-tall orange plastic fencing…and then a cliff. I kid you not. I realized my options were to humble myself, faceplant in front of everyone at the bottom of the mountain, or die. Since I'm writing this book, I'm sure you can guess which option I chose. After that, I learned my lesson and was determined to find the real bunny slopes to figure out how to stop.

Discipling our kids would be so much easier if our parents had intentionally modeled it for us. Maybe that's your story. Maybe your parents modeled discipleship your whole life. That's incredible! But most of us are on the slopes, trying to figure it out without eating snow.

This is why I believe so many parents avoid discipling their kids, hoping a pastor or youth leader will step in and do it for them. I'm not saying this in judgment. I understand the temptation. But we need to recognize that this is our role. We're no longer alone on the slopes, and at some point, we need to learn how to ski so we can teach them too.

> **Not knowing how to disciple and choosing not to disciple are two different things.**

Before Jesus ascended, He met with the eleven disciples (sorry, Judas) on the side of a mountain. This is the moment when our commission to make disciples is given. It's a pivotal moment where Jesus gives us His marching orders as we charge forward with Him, taking ground for His kingdom. This commission wasn't just for these disciples but for every follower of Christ. Though many of us have heard the call—or at least seen the signs as we drive by our local church—we often overlook and forget the verse just before. The verse goes like this: *"The disciples saw Jesus and worshipped Him, but some doubted"* (Matthew 28:17).

That's right. Just before Jesus commissions them—after He had risen from the dead—some of the men He would use to establish His church were still caught doubting. Jesus didn't scold them for their doubts or tell them to do better. He gave them the work that needed to be done.

Don't let your doubts leave you stuck on the ski lift. Jesus, in not so many words, says: you can trust Me, or you can trust your doubts. Not knowing how to disciple and choosing not to disciple are two different things.

Don't let the current of your doubts determine your path. Feelings of inadequacy and disqualification are tools of the enemy, designed to distract us so that we lose our footing and are swept downriver. The disciples felt the same way. But they didn't let their doubts dictate their direction.

At some point, we all feel unprepared for intentional parenting. The difference lies in how we respond and the direction we choose to take.

The truth is, most ski instructors were never Olympic athletes. The majority of them simply love to ski. It is that passion that has made them pretty decent at it. And that's the point: you don't need to be a pastor or a theological expert to disciple your children. Jesus built His entire ministry on the backs of a few fishermen, tax collectors, and sinners, not because they were the best, but because they were passionate about spreading the Gospel of Jesus.

Most of us become paralyzed by our lack of knowledge, which leads us to inaction. The biggest requirement for discipling your child is a love for Jesus that is actively transforming your heart into His image! It can be easy to avoid the slopes to prevent a hard crash. But that's not why you're reading this book. You're reading because you realize there's too much at stake.

Your discipleship journey doesn't have to be the story of your children. Will we crash? Magnificently. I'm talking skis sticking out of the snow, fifty feet apart. And then we swallow our pride (and some snow), pick up our skis, and get back on the lift.

This brings us back to you: The first step in discipling your children is simple—be a disciple yourself.

In Matthew 4:19 we see Jesus' definition of a disciple. Jesus says, "Follow me, and I will make you fishers of men."

A disciple is someone who is:

- Following Jesus ("Follow me")
- Being Changed by Jesus ("I will make you")
- Committed to the mission of Jesus ("fishers of men")

If we are active disciples of Christ, we follow His words and ways, being transformed into His image. In other words, we spend time with Him, learning how to ski. As we grow, we become more committed to His mission of making disciples (Matthew 28:18-20), and we begin teaching others to ski, as well.

Discipling others has never been about always knowing the way ahead. In fact, I've found that the more I know, the less I seem to have figured out. Discipleship is about having a deep love for God that changes us and compels us to share that love with others. As we take steps against the current, we begin to worry less about crashing and focus more on the One who is leading the way. And as we follow Him, there's a good chance there are kid-sized ski tracks close behind.

His Heartbeat

When Lilla was a baby, she had colic. I'm not sure if all colic is created equal, but if there's a worse kind, she had it. During Jennie's pregnancy, we prayed over the qualities we hoped our little girl would have. Passionate was our most frequent request—and passion is exactly what we got. The moral of the story: be specific when you pray. Those first four months were sleepless and filled with relentless, passionate crying. We tried everything. I played running water sounds in the background and experimented with a strange walk-bounce technique. Jennie would nurse, and I even created a playlist of Christian rap songs called "Baby Rap" (which Lilla still enjoys to this day). No matter what we did, nothing seemed to work. We were completely exhausted and out of ideas.

One night, Lilla woke up at 4 a.m., and it was my turn to get up. I dragged myself out of bed, praying this would be quick, but after forty-five minutes, nothing had changed. So, I did. I stopped trying to put her back to sleep and instead put on some worship music, opened the Word, and spent time with my Dad (the heavenly one). The crazy thing is, as soon as I sat down with Jesus, holding my little girl against my chest, she stopped crying. And it wrecked me because that's exactly how it should be.

It shouldn't be music, white noise, or distractions that bring me peace. It should be that I am so close to my Dad that I can hear the beat of His heart. When you're that close to your Heavenly Father, you feel loved, rest comes easy, and monsters don't seem so scary. And when I can't hear His heartbeat, I should be desperate to return to that steady, reliable rhythm. My daughter has been teaching me about Jesus long before she could speak.

You and I were created to be deeply and passionately in love with God. Anytime we find ourselves living apart from that love, it should drive us to do whatever it takes to return to it. The hard truth is, I can't "book" you into falling in love with Jesus. Nothing I say, do, or write in these pages can make that happen for you. What I can do is point you in His direction. I can share what He's done for me, how He's transformed my heart and life. But the journey is yours to take. And love always begins with relationship.

Let me explain. I know about Arnold Schwarzenegger. I know he used to be a shredded weightlifter. I've seen plenty of the movies he's starred in. I even know a little about his time as the Governator (which I'm pretty sure was his official title). But here's the thing, as much as I know about him, I don't know him…and he doesn't know me. We've never met, never crossed paths. There's no relationship. For many Christians, this is how we approach our relationship with God. We know a lot about Him. We know what He did and can quote some things He said. We check all the boxes, follow His commands, and feel like we're doing it right. We know He's not a kindergarten teacher, and we know how to stop Skynet. We know about Arnold! We know about God! But here's the real question: Do you know Him?

For some of us, we've spent our whole lives learning about God without ever starting a relationship with Him.

In Matthew 7:21-23, Jesus says,

"Not everyone who says to Me, 'Lord, Lord,' shall enter the kingdom of heaven, but he who does the will of My Father in heaven. Many will say to Me in that day, 'Lord, Lord, have we not prophesied in Your name, cast out demons in Your name, and done many wonders in Your name?' And then I will declare to them, 'I never knew you; depart from Me, you who practice lawlessness!'"

We don't serve a checkbox Jesus, where performing our way into good standing is the goal. Jesus spoke to people who did all the "Jesus-y things" but didn't do them with Him. His response was unmistakable:

I NEVER KNEW YOU.

Intentional discipleship in your home starts with your own heart. To know God is to love God. Love is the natural response our souls are designed to have when we come into fellowship with Jesus.

Take the Pharisees, for example. They were the religious leaders of their time, and they loved twisting God's law for their own benefit. They knew the law, understood its truth, and checked all the boxes, but they completely missed the point. They didn't know Jesus, and because they didn't know Him, they couldn't love Him. Instead, they loved themselves and their own power.

For some, this might be the very reason God led you to open this book. This could be your starting point, the place where you begin to grow and cultivate a deep, abiding relationship with Jesus.

The beautiful thing about loving Jesus is that His love pulls us toward others who love Him, too. There's a gravity to His love that we can't escape, and, honestly, we don't want to.

Generally speaking, people talk about the things they love most. It's a simple truth. If you love cars, you talk about cars. If you love cooking, you swap recipes. I love my wife, daughter, and the parenting journey, so naturally, I wrote this book about it. When we love something deeply, it naturally comes out in our conversations.

If you're deeply in love with God, the people around you will know it, and it will spark movement in your life. But let's be clear: this isn't about creating a tally of how many times you mention God in your daily conversations to prove your love for Him. That's not the point.

Imagine me coming home and saying to my wife, "Can you believe it? I talked about you seventeen times today!" She'd probably look at me like I'm crazy and ask why I'm keeping count. It's not about quotas or checklists. The point is that it naturally shows when we love something or someone. It's a symptom of love: we talk about the things we care about most.

This applies to God, too! If you're wondering whether God loves you, just open His Word. He can't stop talking about the people He created and His immense love for them. Even though we constantly mess up, God's pursuit of our hearts always outpaces our failures. The Israelites recognized this in Nehemiah 9:16-20a

"But they, our ancestors, became arrogant and stiff-necked, and they did not obey your commands. They refused to listen and failed to remember the miracles you performed among them. They became stiff-necked and in their rebellion appointed a leader in order to return to their slavery. But you are a forgiving God, gracious and compassionate, slow to anger and abounding in love. Therefore you did not desert them, even

when they cast for themselves an image of a calf and said, 'This is your god, who brought you up out of Egypt,' or when they committed awful blasphemies.

Because of your great compassion you did not abandon them in the wilderness. By day the pillar of cloud did not fail to guide them on their path, nor the pillar of fire by night to shine on the way they were to take. You gave your good Spirit to instruct them."

The beauty of this passage lies in the Israelites' acknowledgment of their own straying and the realization that God's faithfulness wasn't dependent on theirs. We serve a God who loves to the extreme, offering each of us the chance to become recipients of that love as adopted children of royalty. His love for us leads us to love Him (1 John 4:19).

If we want families that deeply love and follow Jesus, it starts with us. Do you know Him? Do you love Him? If not, I encourage you to grow in your time with Jesus. At the end of this book, you'll find resources to help guide you as you work to move what's in your head into your heart. If Jesus is someone you know well, I hope this book becomes a tool to help take the love in your heart and move it to your hands and feet as you intentionally disciple your children.

Parenting is not easy, and being intentional requires an even greater sacrifice. You are moving against the current. But everything feels a little more manageable when your head is pressed against your Father's chest. As you grow in your love for Him, I pray your ears ache to hear the rhythm of His heartbeat and that, as you listen to it, you are reminded that you are never alone.

The Fridge is Full

A friend recently shared a thought-provoking question: What would you do if you visited a friend's house and immediately noticed something was off? The moment they opened the door, you saw their sunken face and noticed they'd lost a lot of weight (and not in a healthy way). They were practically skin and bones.

As they shuffled toward the couch, you abandoned polite small talk and asked, point-blank, "Hey, what's going on? You don't look so good. Are you okay?"

Clearly exhausted from their voyage to the door, they took a deep breath before answering. "Honestly, I'm starving. I haven't eaten in weeks." Alarmed, you spring to your feet and rush to the fridge. When you open it, you're stunned to find it fully stocked—meats, drinks, cheeses, and every good thing you can imagine fill every shelf. Dumbfounded, you call out to your friend, "Why haven't you eaten anything?" With a weary sigh, they reply, "Because no one has fed me."

Crazy story, right? Who would ever let themselves reach such a desperate point of starvation?

We would.

Jesus, in His kindness, often uses physical realities to teach spiritual truths. And our spiritual food is clear: it's the Word of God.

I know what you're thinking: "Isn't this a book about discipling my kids?" Yes, it is. But here's the thing: you can only lead someone as far as you've gone yourself. And many of us are spiritually exhausted, starving, and standing just feet away from a fully stocked fridge.

This is one of those "put your own oxygen mask on first" situations. We must feed ourselves first to be equipped to feed others. Our children don't need spiritually malnourished parents attempting to disciple them. We can't afford to become yet another underfed family in a spiritually impoverished world. We don't need to perpetuate a cycle that leaves us hungry and wanting. Your soul needs nourishment. The fridge is full. It's time to feed yourself!

My first two years trying to follow Jesus were rocky, at best. I was learning about Him but not actually following Him.

At one point, I was attending three different churches on different days. I served on Sundays, attended a Bible study on Tuesdays, and participated in a couple of young adult ministries throughout the week. I was doing all the "right" things but starving spiritually.

None of those church services were bad in and of themselves. They were great ministries that have had a significant kingdom impact. The problem was that I didn't truly know Jesus. And because I didn't know Him, I had no idea how to spend time with Him. The spiritual food was being dropped in my lap, but like a newborn, I had no idea how to eat it.

But in one night, everything changed. A friend showed me how to read His Word and what to do with it. For the first time, I began a deep relationship with Jesus. I found a community that pursued me, wanting to know my heart, even the ugly parts.

I was discipled by a man who led me closer to God, challenged me, mentored me as a leader, and showed me how to be a godly man, husband, and dad, one who messes up regularly but is forgiven and loved.

Your ability to disciple your kids is directly tied to your connection with Jesus.

For two years, I didn't mature. The only thing that grew was my hunger. Then, someone showed me the fridge, and I couldn't get enough.

My relationship with Jesus is the best gift I have to offer my family, friends, and the ministries I lead.

In John 15:4-5, Jesus was with His eleven disciples when He said, "Remain in me, as I also remain in you. No branch can bear fruit by itself; it must remain in the vine. Neither can you bear fruit unless you remain in me. I am the vine; you are the branches. If you remain in me and I in you, you will bear much fruit; apart from me, you can do"… a little bit. No. You can do things as long as they have

Jesus vibes? Nope. "Nothing." Your ability to disciple your kids is directly tied to your connection with Jesus.

Imagine telling your family that you had a plan to be everything they ever needed. You'd wake up each day, go to work, come home, take care of them, and eat absolutely nothing. But don't worry. Every Sunday, you'd go to your favorite restaurant and eat your heart out for an hour or so. Come on, this is what you and your stretchy pants have trained for!

What would your family say? Probably something like, "Are you crazy? You can't eat just once a week! That's a terrible idea!" And they'd be right. No one in their right mind would starve themselves like that.

Your relationship with Jesus, your spiritual maturity, and your family's experience with God all begin with the realization that you need to eat daily. No matter how wonderful, Sunday church gatherings are not enough to sustain you.

Your ability to lead your family, minister to your community, or do anything of kingdom value begins with getting up in the morning with your Creator and spending time with Him in His Word.

Let's call this what it really is: a problem. It's easy to be drawn away from the time our souls desperately need, focusing instead on lesser things.

We need to lead ourselves to resist the drift and move toward spiritual nourishment. Leading your family begins with leading yourself. The victory comes when hungry eyes watch as you feed yourself, hoping you'll show them how to open the fridge.

Reflection

1. How is your relationship with Jesus?
a. Pause and truly think about your answer. Do you have a love for Him, or is He just someone you know about?
b. How is your time with Him? Is it active and intentional or casual and occasional?

2. Do you know how to feed yourself? In other words, what does your time in the Bible look like?
a. Are you growing and maturing as a disciple, or have you become stagnant?
b. What does it look like for you to have daily meals with Jesus?

If you are starting out, there is a tool in the resource section of this book called the "SOAP Method" that can help!

Challenge

Find a way to prioritize your time with Jesus—and follow through. If I don't schedule time with Him tomorrow, it simply won't happen. Don't be afraid to use your calendar. You'd schedule an appointment or meeting. You can schedule your quiet time too. When will you meet with Him tomorrow? What will it look like? Make a plan, invite your community to come alongside you—and stick to it. It might take a little time to find the right rhythm that works with your current season of life. Don't give up if the first time doesn't work out as planned. Stay committed and intentional to meeting with Jesus.

Zooming In

When it comes to discipling the next generation, it's easy to assume that it requires a perfect home life, endless free time, and a seminary degree. But the truth is, discipleship happens in the everyday moments—around the dinner table, in the car on the way to school, at bedtime, or even during a quick run to the grocery store. It's not about having the perfect family structure; it's about being intentional with the influence you *do* have.

For some, discipleship happens in a home with two parents who share the responsibility. But for many, that's not the reality. If you're a single parent, a grandparent stepping into a parental role, or someone raising kids in a blended family, we see you. We know you may not have chosen this path—whether through loss, betrayal, or circumstances beyond your control. The road you're walking is not easy, but you don't have to walk alone, and your role in discipling your children is just as powerful.

Throughout Scripture, we see God working through all kinds of family structures. Timothy, one of the early church leaders, was discipled primarily by his mother and grandmother (2 Timothy 1:5). Jesus Himself was raised by Joseph, his adoptive earthly father. The church has always been a place where spiritual mothers, fathers, siblings, and mentors step in to help form the faith of the next generation.

So whether you are discipling your child alone, co-parenting from different homes, or figuring out how to blend a new family together, take heart—God's design for discipleship has never depended on the "ideal" family situation. What matters most is consistency, presence, and a willingness to model a life surrendered to Jesus. And remember, you don't have to do this alone. The church is your family too, and we are here to walk with you.

No matter your household dynamic, you have been placed in your child's life for a reason. God can and will use you to shape their faith in ways you may not even realize. Keep showing up, keep pointing them to Jesus in the small moments, and trust that God is doing a work in your home—whatever it looks like.

The Magnifying Glass

When Jennie and I got married, we were showered with gifts. People went above and beyond to show us love. I even got a Batman piggy bank, though Jennie wasn't a fan. We couldn't have been more grateful (well, maybe minus the piggy bank—seriously, Jennie hated it).

But the greatest gift I received that day came from Jesus, a tiny, invisible magnifying glass that only I knew about. No, I'm not saying I had some dramatic Damascus-road moment where Jesus appeared, shouting, "Come! Look at things closer!"

I'm saying that through my marriage, Jesus gave me a way to look deeper into my heart. My marriage quickly became a magnifying glass…and I didn't like what I saw very much. Before we married, I considered myself a pretty selfless guy. But once we were married, that magnifying glass made it painfully clear just how self-centered I really was.

To be clear, there's a fairly decent chance that your family and my family don't look exactly the same. Some of you have all the kids, while others might be expecting. Some are married, while others navigate single parenthood, and still others walk the tightrope of co-parenting. Marriage is a magnifying glass, but so is parenting. God has provided every single one of us with a way to look closer at how we can become more like Him.

For me, there were—and still are—so many things in my heart that needed to be cut away for me to become the husband Jennie deserves and the man I was created to be. It wasn't pretty, and learning to grow as a servant wasn't my favorite process.

Little did I know another magnifying glass would arrive less than two years later, the day our daughter was born. That's the kindness of Jesus. Instead of overwhelming me with all my brokenness at once, and leaving me to choke on my failure, He reveals it in manageable, bite-sized chunks. He gives me just enough to zoom in a little further, shaping me to become more like Him, which brings me to what you've probably already figured out: marriage and kids don't solve your problems. They magnify them. In fact, both are likely to make you more aware of your issues than ever. They reveal the deep, ugly heart issues hidden within, and let's be honest, heart surgery is never pleasant.

Yet, as I've used my magnifying glass to allow God to identify and cut away the ugly parts of my heart, I've also seen it magnify His glory. That's the kind of marriage I long for, one that models the Gospel for our kids and brings praise to God.

Of course, Jennie is married to me, so she has to deal with plenty of my stumbling along the way. But step by step, our marriage keeps striving to lift God's name higher and higher. This starts with you, especially if your spouse isn't a disciple of Jesus. Here's the wonderful part: your magnifying glass wasn't created for you to become the fruit inspector of your spouse. This isn't about how they fall short. This is about you doing your part to grow as a disciple and, if you're married, to lead out health in your marriage. Is it better if they are believers? Yes! Pray for that day to come, but know that you can only do your part, and right now, your part is to clear your side of the road.

The beauty of magnifying glasses is that they don't just reveal the negative. They also help us zoom in on the Kingdom victories happening in our hearts. A healthy marriage is a key step in discipling your kids through the challenges and joys.

Although a healthy marriage is important, it's not the only path. If you are married, I double-emphasize everything I just wrote. Your marriage has a direct impact on your kiddos. But if you're not married, I need you to hear this. We see you. We see the difficult mornings, getting the kids ready for school so you can barely make it to work on time. We see you carry more than any one person was ever meant to lift, and you do it with grace. We see you fighting for your family even at your own expense. We see you, and you're not alone.

My prayer is that your magnifying glass will help you zoom in on how you can grow as a disciple of Jesus. The closer you are to Him, the better a parent you will be.

The difficulty is that drift happens most in our priorities, regardless of family dynamics. Most of us have a short memory, prioritizing what's most recent and most visible. This often shapes how we organize the hierarchy of our lives. We fall in love with Jesus, then marry someone, and eventually have kids, discovering a whole new dimension of love. While this was God's ideal path for families, we know many roads can lead you to this book! Recency and visibility often dictate our priorities so that our priorities look like this:

1. Kids
2. Spouse
3. God

If you want, you could sprinkle in work, hobbies, your fantasy football league, and friends as other priorities that we love to put in the wrong places. A disciple of Jesus needs to know and pursue the proper order.

In 2015, I traveled to North Carolina with a very specific goal: I was going to ask Jennie's parents for their blessing to "put a ring on it." Excited and a little nervous, I couldn't help but feel the weight of the moment. We'd only been dating for about ten months, and while I was sure Jennie would say yes, I wasn't as confident about her parents.

Her parents loved me (and still do), and we got along great. But they had seen her heart broken before and were understandably protective. Determined to make a good impression, I stopped at a gas station to get dressed up. I felt like Superman in a phone booth. I even put on a tie so they'd know I meant business.

When I arrived, I sat them down on the couch and asked the question I'd been rehearsing in my head: "I love your daughter with all my heart and intend to continue loving her for the rest of my life. May I have your blessing to marry her?"

Jennie's mom looked at me and asked just one question—the most important question she could have asked. "Do you love Jesus more than you love my daughter?" Without hesitation, I looked at her sincerely and said, "Yes."

I love the irony of gaining their blessing by telling my future in-laws that their daughter would always be in second place. And yet, that is exactly where she belongs. Placing her anywhere else would burden her with a role she was never meant to fulfill. My wife is incredible, but she makes a terrible god. Jennie knows she is not my number one priority, and here's a little secret: I'm not hers either. Many failed marriages stem from misplaced priorities. When both spouses keep Jesus as their first priority and their marriage as their second, it becomes incredibly difficult for that marriage to end in divorce.

Our kids hold our hearts, but they don't belong in first or second place. Jesus is number one. He never falls off of His throne, and He doesn't wear Burger King crowns. He is King, and His chair isn't meant to be shared with anyone. If you're married, your spouse is number two—your ride or die—your partner in crime. By design, our kids are meant to come third.

Here's an easy reason why (one I try not to think about as often as possible): one day, our children are going to leave us. That's just the reality of how this works. They are disciples, raised to be sent out. My marriage comes before my kids, and they are blessed because of it. This is why, when Lilla speaks rudely to Jennie, I address it by reminding her that she cannot speak to my wife that way. In that moment, Jennie isn't just her mom. She's my bride, and my bride is the priority. It's an opportunity for my daughter to see that Jennie and I are a team.

Co-parenting adds another layer of complexity to this concept, yet it remains just as crucial. As a Student Pastor, I've seen far too many kiddos become the proverbial rope in their parents' tug-of-war. Trying to win your kids over by undermining their other parent doesn't serve them. It hurts them. He may no longer be your husband, but he is still their dad. She may not be your wife, but she is still Mom. Prioritizing a cooperative, respectful relationship—wherever possible—is in your children's best interest and ultimately benefits you, too. How you speak about their other parent, even in the face of hurt and betrayal, teaches your kids more than you realize. Choose words that reflect kindness and respect, even when they are not being reciprocated, because whether you intend to or not, you are always teaching them something.

Prioritizing your marriage or alignment with a co-parent teaches kids that unity is foundational, both for our family and for future relationships.

Our priorities were always meant to be in this order:

1. God
2. Spouse
3. Kids

We need to use the magnifying glass to examine our hearts and ensure our priorities align with God's design. The beauty of making God the priority is this: the closer my wife and I individually grow to Him, the closer we grow as a couple. The same is true for our kids. It is Jesus who draws us closer together in relationship and love.

That said, let me clarify what I mean by priority. It's easy to compartmentalize our lives into a rigid hierarchy, but that's not the point. Prioritizing Jesus isn't about simply reading your Bible in the morning and attending church on Sundays. It's about making Him first in everything—our thoughts, actions, and relationships.

When we think about our top three priorities, it's not like dividing a pie chart into separate time segments. Instead, imagine interconnected circles overlapping in every area of our lives.

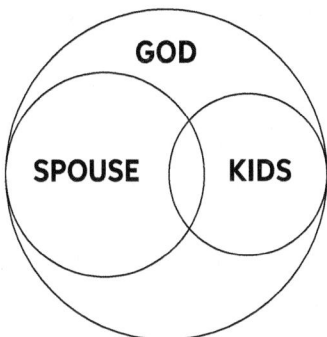

God isn't meant to occupy just a portion of your heart. The command is to love Him with all your heart. He isn't just the God of morning devotionals or Sunday services. He's an all-encompassing God who desires to be part of every moment of my day.

When I love my wife well, it's through the strength Jesus provides. When I disciple my kids intentionally, it's His guidance leading me. I don't set aside one priority for another. Instead, I bring all my priorities into my relationship with Jesus. As life pulls us in different directions, careers and hobbies often creep in and take precedence where they shouldn't. When work or hobbies take priority over our relationship with God, our spouse, or our kids, the relationships that matter most begin to feel like obstacles. Do you view your family as a distraction from what you want? Is your time with God starting to feel like a chore? Does your spouse seem to interrupt your fun or downtime?

When your top three priorities start competing with lesser things, division and disunity take root in your heart. If this resonates with you, the issue isn't your spouse or family. It's a signal to check your heart.

I get it. This is easier said than done, and I don't want anyone to think that this is something that I have figured out. I make my share of mistakes and have had more drift than I'd like to admit. We just need to know what it should look like so we can continue moving in the right direction. If there are parts of your life that you have boxed Jesus out of, now is the time to invite Him in and hit the reset button on your priorities. He is the only shot that you and I have at being the spouses and parents that we were created to be because in all of it, more than anything, we were created to be with Him.

As our circles shift from God to gymnastics competitions and marriage vows to parenting, we often forget an important truth: *Parents are meant to be teammates, not roommates.* When you demote your spouse on your priority list, you also demote their place in your heart. You stop connecting and start forgetting that connection needs to be pursued. Remember when you were dating? When everything was exciting, and you couldn't wait to surprise your partner with something extravagant? Why did you stop? It's a slow drift in priorities that you didn't notice until it became obvious. Some of you need to set this book down right now and lavish your spouse with a spontaneous act of love. Just because they're yours doesn't mean they don't need to be pursued. You are meant to be on the same team, and parenting serves as a magnifying glass to reveal whether you're moving together against the current or if you're being pulled downstream.

For Jennie and me, the test has been very real. We were constantly confronted with differences of opinion on bedtime routines, discipline, whether organic really matters (but seriously... does it?), and much more. There were seasons when it felt like we couldn't agree on anything, and the problem was we were both certain that we were one hundred percent right. By all accounts, we were a dysfunctional team. And as dysfunction continued, we stopped functioning as a team altogether. We stopped fighting for each other, and there wasn't much fighting against each other either. We became two tired individuals, simply trying to coexist. This is where every marriage has the potential to go if we aren't careful. Jesus wants more for your marriage.

The truth is love is a choice. Let's set aside all the fairytale nonsense and get real. Love is something you have to choose. When our priorities shift, we stop making that intentional choice. There was never a moment in my relationship with Jennie when she didn't want to be pursued and showered with love. After all, she claims an entire month for her birthday. She loves being lavished upon, and if I'm honest, so do I. We all have a God-given desire to be seen, valued, appreciated, and loved. But when our priorities shift, our pursuit drifts away from our marriage and gets focused on lesser things. Your job? Lesser. Your hobbies? Lesser. Your video games? Lesser. Your financial status? Lesser. We must remember that while we may be married, we were never meant to stop dating. Date your spouse. Choose your spouse. The pursuit doesn't stop when kids arrive. Does it change? Yes. Absolutely! Things are different. Is it harder? One hundred percent. But that doesn't change the fact that a marriage that swims against the current is so worth it.

Dating your spouse is a step, but alignment is essential. As parents, it's crucial that you're on the same page, not making up the rules as you go. You won't be prepared for everything, but there's a lot you can prepare for. The real challenge, though, is that many of us have lost the art of conversation. We often view disagreement as relational treason. "I thought you loved me! You don't trust me in this?" Stop it. Open disagreement is actually a sign of trust, not its absence. Think about it: you'll only openly disagree with someone you trust to handle your perspective and won't jeopardize the relationship over it. When we tiptoe around each other, our fear of rocking the boat keeps us from discussing anything meaningful. Jesus didn't walk on eggshells. He walked on water. He wasn't afraid to make waves as He moved against the current and pursued His bride. Similarly, we must be willing to take risks by having difficult conversations with the goal of unity, not victory.

Here's the problem: I don't want to have a hard conversation when Jennie and I aren't jiving because… well, wisdom. But I also don't want to bring up difficult issues when things are going well because I don't want to ruin a great night. I get the tension, but there's a clear right answer. We need to risk the good to pursue the better. I'd rather have a tough conversation that prevents disunity down the road and risk losing one good night than hold on to that one good night and remain off course. If unity is the true target, I will enter every conversation with humility and love. I will be fearless to own my part and quick to seek forgiveness. This holds true even if they've deeply hurt you. Even if your marriage is over, you're still parenting together. You can only control your part—so do it well. It's about taking the long view, moving intentionally against the current, step by step. You'll pay for the decision you make. The question is: would you prefer to pay now or later? If your marriage is second in your life (after Jesus), the answer becomes clear. It's time to place your marriage where it belongs.

Jesus didn't walk on eggshells. He walked on water.

The Telescope

Although my marriage serves as a magnifying glass for me, it functions as a telescope for our kids. Our marriage and parenting allow our children to look ahead at distant things, showing them what to expect, how they should be treated, and how they should behave. If you're coparenting, this is still true. Here's what

I mean. One random day, while Jennie was at work, I snuck home with roughly nine million feet of string. To anyone who saw me, it probably looked like I was about to embark on a sweater-knitting spree. I tied one end of the string to the laundry room door handle (where she would enter the house), and next to it, I left a note that read, "Follow the string." I masterfully wound the string from room to room around the house like a large, clumsy spider. At each stop, there was a gift—each room held a sweet note, chocolates, a rose, or her favorite wine. Whatever it was, she had to follow the string to get to each item. To this day, I don't know where I saw this romantic gesture, but I know I stole it from somewhere. When Jennie came home, her eyes welled up as she followed the string from one point to another. She felt incredibly cared for, but that wasn't my only goal.

As Jennie followed the string, our daughter trailed behind her, watching as her mom was lavished with love. When Jennie finally reached the end of this romantic journey, she gave me a hug, then knelt down and told our daughter something I will never forget. She looked Lilla in the eyes and said, "This is how a man should treat you."

Our marriage is the first picture of the Gospel that our kids will ever see. Before they can understand, speak, or read, they see us. I want our daughter to witness Jesus' pursuit, love, forgiveness, and kindness in the way I treat her mom. We don't always get it right, but the truth remains: our marriage is the first picture of the Gospel our kids will ever see. Your magnifying glass is their telescope. Through my marriage, I am constantly showing Lilla her incredible worth—or failing to do so. Every day, I demonstrate what it means for a man to cherish and respect a woman. Your marriage carries that same influence!

If you're a single parent, coparenting, or part of a blended family, your role as a telescope is even more direct. Your kids hear and pick up on much more than you might realize. They hear how you talk on the phone to your friends about their other parent. They sense the frustration and anger when things didn't go as you'd hoped…again. While those things may happen, we can't allow hurt, resentment, anger, or bitterness to shift our focus. Perhaps your kids don't have the opportunity to see a loving marriage, but that doesn't mean you can't demonstrate what a loving relationship looks like for them. Take your son or daughter on a date! Establish a rhythm that is both meaningful and sustainable. Show them—through your actions—how they deserve to be treated, that their value is undeniable, and what healthy relationships should look like in their future.

Whether I mean to or not, I am actively demonstrating to Lilla the type of behavior that is acceptable from a man. That's a sobering concept for me as I confront my own sin and struggles. Our life isn't a fairytale, and wonderful gestures of love are often spaced between my own glorious mistakes. But even in that, there's victory. If our marriage is meant to represent the Gospel, then our kids should also see our failures and the redemption stories that follow. Their eyes are watching, and our marriage is teaching something. This is your (and my) chance to use that magnifying glass to inspect your hearts and your marriage, ensuring you're teaching the right message.

Reflection

1. What "current" priorities are most important to you and your family? What needs to change?
a. If married, invite your spouse into this. If you're co-parenting, this is still an important conversation for you to have. Answer separately and then compare the results. What is the same, and what is different? Why?
b. Look at your schedule and budget and the story they tell. If a stranger saw where you spent your money and your time, where would they say your priorities are?

2. How aligned are you with your spouse or co-parent in the following areas:
a. Dating - What does dating your spouse look like in your current life stage?
b. Money - What are your views on spending, giving, saving, and debt?
c. Priorities - After the last question, are you aligned or in disagreement?

3. Are there any areas of disunity that need to be addressed?

4. What is your marriage or co-parenting relationship teaching your child/children about Jesus? Is it a story of grace and blessing or of conflict and disunity?

Challenge

Don't read this book alone! Read it with your spouse, co-parent, family member, or friend! Talk through the concepts together. Press in to create better alignment and direction. If you are a single parent, find another parent you can process this book with.

If married: Plan a date with your spouse. It doesn't need to be expensive; it just needs to be thoughtful and intentional. You and your spouse need kid-free time to grow together. Don't minimize it—prioritize it. Ask questions during the date to establish a healthy rhythm in your relationship. How often do you both need a date night? How often can you have intentional time together at home (after bedtime), and how often will you need a babysitter? Try doing a "Stop, Start, Continue" exercise. Ask your spouse: What am I currently doing that I should stop? What is something I'm not doing that I should start? And what am I doing well that I should continue doing as we move forward?

If single parenting or co-parenting: Plan a date with each of your kids. It doesn't need to be expensive. Most kids are pretty cheap dates! It just needs to be special and intentional. You'd be amazed at how many kids would choose lying under the stars over a fancy meal. Quality time together beats money spent every time. Come prepared with some intentional questions. Pursue their hearts. You are their telescope! Show them the incredible value they have.

A Connection Issue

We've all been there. You jump into the car after a long work day, dreaming of your couch, the game, and your favorite beverage. You can practically taste it. You shove your keys into the ignition, turn them quickly, and… nothing. Not a sound. You try again, hoping it's just a glitch, but no luck. Your car won't start. Frustrated, you text home, declaring that the world is ending, while flagging down the nearest person in hopes they'll give you a jump. You pop the hood and instantly identify the problem: your cables have become disconnected. At that moment, you realize that turning the key would never have worked, using jumper cables would never have worked, or even attempting a push start would never have worked. Nothing could possibly have fixed the issue unless you first reconnected the cables.

This is often how we approach parenting. We see a problem and do everything we know to resolve it. Your child is acting out, so you impose consequences to stop the behavior. You raise your voice to show you're serious. You even celebrate the few times they get it right, but no matter what you do, nothing seems to change long term. You turn the key and…silence. Your volume increases, and so does your frustration. You're at a complete loss. This is the story of so many parents I've had the privilege of walking beside during my time as a pastor. They've come to me, completely exasperated, because they've tried everything they know to do. The irony is that I'm still trying to figure out this intentional parenting thing like everyone else. But what I've found to be true is that when our kids are drifting and struggling, it's often less about consequences or behavior modification and more about a connection issue. That's the problem with focusing on fixing behavior: even if you succeed, you've only addressed the symptom.

Here's what I mean. You go to the doctor and tell him, "Hey Doc, I've got some issues. I'm sweating for no reason, my chest feels tight, and I have this stinging pain radiating down my left arm." Here's what the doctor is not going to do: He's not going to tell you that these are very serious symptoms and that each one needs to be dealt with immediately and individually. He's not going to prescribe staying in the AC all day to alleviate your sweating. He's not going to suggest wearing baggy shirts to help with your chest tightness, and he's certainly not going to give you a pack of ice for your arm pain. If a doctor did that, I've got bad news: there's a very real chance you could die. Any doctor would tell you immediately that these are symptoms of a bigger issue. There's a high probability that you're having a heart attack, and in order for you to have any hope of survival, they need to treat your heart first.

> That's the problem with focusing on fixing behavior: even if you succeed, you've only addressed the symptom.

The problem is that, especially with our kids, behaviors are easy. They're easy to see, easy to address, and sometimes easy to correct. But behavior modification doesn't fix the heart. I'm not arguing against consequences. Consequences are real and should be used wisely and in love. What I'm encouraging parents to do is look beyond the behavior and into the heart. To ask some hard questions like: what's driving this kind of response, habit, or behavior? I guarantee it's a heart issue. And our ability to speak into and shepherd our child's heart comes down to our connection. How is your connection with your child? Are the cables attached to the battery, or are they falling off to the side? I'm not saying this in judgment. I've been there. I've tried to fix poor behavior, only to realize that no changes could be made because our connection wasn't where it needed to be.

Before entering ministry, I taught seventh-grade English. You might wonder what qualifications I had to become an English teacher—honestly, none. I had no qualifications beyond a bachelor's degree and a good attitude.

In my interview (a few weeks after the school year had already begun), I told the Assistant Principal that I didn't plan on teaching for more than a year. I explained that God was calling me into ministry but believed this school could be my mission field for the next ten months.

It was a public school interview, and I was breaking all the rules. I told them I didn't plan to be a long-term teacher, I wasn't qualified, and I even talked about Jesus. Still, they hired me on the spot.

Any pride I felt about that accomplishment faded the moment I walked into my classroom for the first time. The principal leaned in the doorway and whispered, "Good luck, this is the toughest class in the school." And boom. The math checked out. No qualified teacher in their right mind would want to teach this class. So, why not look for someone unqualified? But I wasn't discouraged. I believed God had called me to make a difference in these kids' lives and hearts. I just didn't know how difficult it would be.

A couple of weeks in, and I hated my job. Y'all, I've served in the military, worked as an EMT on an ambulance, and faced the challenges of ministry—but without a doubt, teaching was the toughest job I've ever had. Shout out to all the teachers out there. Y'all are built different.

I dreaded going to work, and my drive home was often spent venting to my wife about how difficult my day had been. In my defense, my classes were tough. It was a Title 1 school, with many students who had already experienced the worst life had to offer. One of my students came in a month after I started because he had been shot. Fights were a daily occurrence (sometimes even in my classroom), and Jesus seemed nowhere to be found.

By November, my pride was the only thing keeping me going. I wish I could say it was Jesus, but the truth is, I just wasn't willing to quit. I wasn't going to let these kids beat me. And then, something happened.

It was a Tuesday night, and I was at our Young Adults Ministry. In the middle of worship, I began praying, "God, change their hearts. God, change their hearts. God, please change their hearts." Then, deep within my chest, I felt the Holy Spirit respond, "You're not here for their hearts. I want to change yours."

I was wrecked. All this time, I had been focused on their behavior while God was holding a scalpel, ready for my own open-heart surgery. I laid down my pride, climbed onto the gurney, and invited Him to do His work.

The next day, because Jesus lavishes His love on me, He gave me an idea. What if this was a connection issue? What if it wasn't about teaching them (I know that's exactly what parents want to hear)? What if English wasn't the point of me being in that room?

At that moment, the Holy Spirit gave me a vision…basketball. They needed to see I was human. I needed a way to connect with them, and I also wanted to show them who was in charge. So, I decided to give up some of my personal time each week to play basketball with a bunch of kids who hated authority.

But discipleship isn't merely organic. It requires intentionality. So, I devised a plan. I picked eight kids who had regular behavior issues in my class. (One had even threatened to punch me in the face.) I also chose one student who had credibility and influence over the others and who was making good choices. Then, I sat with each student individually and shared my plan with them. I told them I was ready to destroy them in basketball, that their tiny 7th-grade bodies were about to be ground into dust. I kid you not; smack talk was like a love language to these guys. This allowed me to start building credibility. I told them we would play every Wednesday after school, but with one condition. I needed grade and behavior reports from their teachers each week to ensure they didn't have any grades lower than a C and weren't causing problems in other classes. They were discouraged, but I wasn't finished.

> **Discipleship isn't merely organic. It requires intentionality.**

As I prayed over the plan, it hit me: these kids had been hearing words like "not good enough," "failure," "broken beyond repair," "abandoned," and "unchosen" their whole lives. I wasn't willing to be just another voice in the chaos. So I continued, "If you have a D or lower, or if you've gotten into trouble that week, you can still play ball with us…BUT only after you first attend tutoring with me that Tuesday. Don't worry, I'm buying us pizza." (Praise God for Little Caesar's $5 Hot-N-Ready).

Back in November, I had all but given up on these kids. But Jesus changed my heart and showed me what it meant to love them intentionally. I needed to meet them where they were.

So often, we expect our kids to behave like adults, to do the right thing, to talk less, or not make a scene. We expect them to be where we are instead of meeting them where they are. Jesus didn't do that. Philippians 2:6 tells us that "[Jesus], being in very nature God, did not consider equality with God something to be used to His own advantage." He didn't wait for us to get our act together before loving us. No. If that's what you took away, you're reading the wrong book. His love for us was so strong that He left His throne in heaven to meet us in our mess. He went from wearing a crown to a diaper as a response to His immense, unstoppable love for us. This was Jesus' model for love.

So why am I so prone to respond louder when someone isn't where I want them to be, as though I can shout them out of their mess and up to my more socially acceptable position? What would happen if we simply met our children where they are?

Relationship and intentionality are the keys. I can't meet my kids where they are if I don't know where they are. We need to pursue our children's hearts in the same way Jesus pursues us, and as we do, it will become clearer and clearer where they stand. During the same school year, I started discipling the teacher across the hall from me. This guy was an amazing teacher but was new to following Jesus.

One morning, before school, during our regular discipleship meeting, he was venting about his mother-in-law. He was frustrated by her behavior, a frustration that was only amplified by the fact that my friend and his family were living in her home. He said, "I don't understand why she acts this way." His frustrations were understandable, but I had some questions.

I asked him if he had ever been involved in his daughter's potty training process. He looked a little confused but answered, "Yes." "So, you've probably changed your fair share of dirty diapers, huh?" He laughed, an obvious "Yes." I then asked if he had ever become angry with his daughter because she made a dirty diaper. He shrugged, saying that while it wasn't convenient, he tried really hard not to get frustrated with her. "Why?" I asked. He responded quickly, "Because she was an infant. It wasn't her fault."

Just before this conversation, we had walked through the different stages of spiritual maturity, and I could see the realization dawn on him. I asked, without judgment, "Where is your mother-in-law in her walk with Jesus?" "She's probably a spiritual infant," he responded. Why do we get so frustrated when our kids, the competing cart in the grocery store, or the other car at the traffic light do something we don't like? It's because we expect them to act how we want them to. We have a "no dirty diapers allowed" sign on our hearts. But what if they are infants? What if they are spiritually dead? What if they don't know any better and need someone to meet them where they are, to give them what they need to mature?

I'm not saying we don't offer accountability. But there is a significant difference between a mess created by an infant and one created by a young adult. A capable young adult needs to clean up their mess. They know better and know how to clean it themselves. But an infant needs help, love, and encouragement as you guide them into maturity. Discipline and cleaning messes aren't the only implications here. When I know where my child is, I also know what she needs to grow and what she needs to eat.

In 1 Corinthians 3:2, Paul says, *"I gave you milk, not solid food, for you were not yet ready for it. Indeed, you are still not ready."* Paul is saying that he wanted to give them meat, but giving steak to a baby is irresponsible and invites them to choke. Knowing where your kids are spiritually will tell you exactly what they need to grow.

Your kids are not spiritual adults yet, and maybe neither are you. That's okay. The incredible thing is as you guide your child toward spiritual maturity, you'll find yourself growing with them. They're likely spiritually dead, infants, or children. Physical age doesn't directly determine their level of maturity. I've known spiritual infants who've known Christ the majority of their lives and spiritual parents who've only been following Christ for a short time. It all comes down to their walk with Jesus.

As the primary disciple-maker of your kids, your job is to identify where they are, meet them there, and give them what they need to grow.

Your job is to identify where they are, meet them there, and give them what they need to grow.

As I continued to play basketball with my students, I noticed things had shifted. The biggest change was that I genuinely loved my students. I loved them. I looked forward to seeing them every day, excited to tell them how I was going to get six blocks this Wednesday instead of the meager five I had the week before. Yes, I'm 6'2", and no, there was no mercy. I used tutoring and basketball as opportunities to build relationships with these kids, to get to know their lives, and to share what Jesus was doing in my heart. Admittedly, not all of them changed. Some kids were still making the same choices, but others started to make a shift. By this point, other teachers were joining in. They were asking what I was doing to change these kids. They started playing basketball, sitting in on tutoring sessions, and even providing the pizza. One student approached me and said that spring had been the first semester that he had no grades lower than a C. Another told me he didn't sleep through his standardized testing because he wanted to make me proud. Even more, students were working hard to be more respectful toward their teachers.

When the standardized test results came back, my students dramatically improved in nearly every area! They were thriving, and I can't overemphasize how little I knew about being an English teacher! I literally failed the teacher's test three times. I knew nothing. I'm not a school teacher, and honestly, teaching them English wasn't even close to being my top priority. Despite all that, these kids were improving in all subjects. All I did was meet them where they were and offer them a bit of my relationship with Jesus, which made all the difference.

When there's a connection issue, it's not the battery that goes to the cable to get connected. Instead, the cable must meet the battery where it is. As intentional, discipling parents, we need to remember that our kids don't need parents who call out, "Climb better. You need to get up to where I am. Act like an adult." Our kids need parents who, like Jesus, step down into the mess to show them they are loved and not alone and that climbing together is far more rewarding than shouting from the top of a mountain.

Tell Them Who They Are

My wife, Jennie, is a kindergarten teacher. I know. My compliment to teachers might seem a bit self-serving, but I truly meant it. She teaches at a school facing immense challenges with students desperately in need of love and encouragement. Jennie, who is naturally more compassionate than I am, prioritizes meeting her kids where they are emotionally and mentally. But she doesn't stop there. In her classroom, she has a mirror surrounded by words that frame it—words like "loved," "chosen," "kind," "smart," and "brave." There are about ten of them in total. Each week, when her students enter the room, she brings them to the mirror, selects a word that fits each child, and encourages them to speak it aloud. As they look into the mirror, seeing their own reflection, they say things like, "I am brave." Every word is carefully chosen. Jennie's method: meet the kids where they are, but speak into who they can become.

Too often, our words communicate things to our kids that we never intended. *You're not good enough. You mess up all the time. You don't deserve love.* And even if we don't say these words outright, what matters more is what they hear. I find myself asking: Who am I telling my daughter that she is? This goes beyond simply what they hear—it's about the message we reinforce. In his book *Everybody Always*, Bob Goff says, "People become who you tell them they are." [1] We get so caught up in focusing on what people are doing that we forget to remind them of who they are meant to be. But God doesn't make that mistake.

I met Andrew one night at our student ministry. He and his brother were sitting in the lobby during small group time. I asked them if they knew where their group was, but Andrew wasn't interested in me. He wasn't shy about letting me know he didn't care who I was or what I wanted. I could have pulled the authority card, but something felt off. Instead of taking them to their group, I spent the next twenty minutes joking around with Andrew and his brother, working on building a connection. Slowly, I saw walls starting to come down. Not long after, Andrew agreed to meet with me every week for discipleship. We'd talk about the struggles in his life and where Jesus was in the midst of it all. As I discipled him, I began bringing him along with me. I'll never forget the day I picked him up from his house, planning to show him how to love others well. We were on our way to the local grocery store, where I was going to pick out flowers for my wife, and he was going to get some for his mom. As we drove, I noticed Sharpie markings on his arm. I knew enough of his story to suspect what they were, but I wanted him to tell me. I asked him about the markings, and after some hesitation, he finally shared. They were gang signs representing the gang his father was involved in—and the same one Andrew hoped to join.

At that moment, I silently prayed. I needed my next words to be intentional and clear, reflecting Jesus rather than my own frustration. Everything inside me wanted to react—to shout how crazy this was, how he needed to wake up, and how he had no idea what he was getting into. But deep down, I felt the Holy Spirit urging me toward a completely different response.

---

[1] Bob Goff, *Everybody, Always: Becoming Love in a World Full of Setbacks and Difcult People* (Nashville: Thomas Nelson, 2018), 35.

I asked him, "Who are you?" He pointed to his arm, his voice calm, and said, "This is who I want to be." I paused, not wanting to rush in with my response. "You think so little of yourself," I said gently. "You believe the best you can achieve is just membership, but that's a lie. It's like me defining my worth by being a pastor. If I did that, I'd be thinking too little of myself, too. Don't you know you were made for royalty?" I could tell he didn't know how to respond, but there was a shift in his expression—he seemed open. So, I kept pressing. I told him he was chosen, bought at a price, and everything else was a lie. My heart longed for him to finally see himself the way Jesus saw him. We continued meeting each week for a few more months until he moved across the state to live with his dad. I wish this story had a happier ending. I pray that conversation planted seeds in his heart and that someday, he'll realize who he was created to be. I hope that by speaking life over him, he'll one day believe it for himself... but I may never know.

In the book of Judges, things were not going well for Israel. The Israelites had been at the mercy of the Midianites for seven years and were in dire straits. But in His mercy, God decided to do something about it. He sent an angel to a man named Gideon with a message: "The Lord is with you, mighty warrior." Did you catch that? The focus wasn't on who Gideon was or what he had already done. According to Gideon, he was from the weakest clan, and the least in his family. Everything pointed to the fact that Gideon was anything but a mighty warrior. He was the runt of the litter, perhaps even a coward. But God looked past who he was and spoke to who he would become. He wasn't meant to be the lowest member of a weak family—he was made for battle. So are our children. So are the kids in Jennie's classroom and even the ones in the toy store throwing a tantrum. Each of us is meant to prepare for battle. And part of that preparation is speaking life into our kids. So, how are you doing? What words are you speaking over your kids? How well are you doing at telling your kids who they are meant to become?

This isn't just about words. It's also about how we choose to speak. One night, my buddy Chase was over at my house, and Lilla was supposed to be going to bed, but she was testing her limits and pushing back. I asked her to come over, and we talked about it. At the time, I didn't think much of the conversation, but later, Chase brought it up. He said he had watched her push back, and what stood out to him was that my entire conversation with her was wrapped in respect. She was acting like a child, but I spoke to her as if she was much older. I maintained eye contact, spoke with gentleness, and treated her with respect. When we feel disrespected, our natural response is often to mirror that disrespect. When we feel unloved, we can respond by withholding love. But that's not how Jesus responds. My daughter's behavior doesn't change who she was created to be, so her disrespect doesn't justify me disrespecting her. This story stuck out to Chase because as I respected her, and in return, she began responding to me with respect.

It's so easy to focus on what we see or hear and to become frustrated. But instead, we should meet our kids where they are and tell them who they will become. Is that where you are right now? Do you feel frustrated as your kids grumble about simple chores, your three-year-old turns the walls into a canvas with crayons, or your teenager retreats to his room?

The natural response is to correct them by telling them to act like an adult, pointing out how they're messing up, and matching their level of disrespect. But remember, we are swimming against the current to create something new. As we work to build a deeper connection with our children, we need to focus on three key things:

1. Meet them where they are.
2. Tell them who they will become.
3. And speak as though they already are.

If we prioritize these three things, we create a healthy space for God to work in their hearts. The best part is that significant change can begin with a single conversation. This kind of movement against the current transforms kids into disciples as they look in the mirror and hear you tell them who they are.

Take Them with You

When I started my first ministry job as a Young Adults pastor, the guy discipling me and this book's coauthor, Matt, shared something I can't seem to shake. He said, "Just about everything you do, you shouldn't do alone." These weren't just words to him—they were a principle he lived by. He meant that, when planning curriculum and content, I had leaders who would love to speak into it—people with more experience eager to help me craft the ministry's new greeting strategy. At one point, he even told me that I shouldn't spend too much time in the office and that I needed to be out, engaging with people. If I'm going somewhere, I shouldn't go alone. I've taken this to heart and applied it, especially in how I intentionally disciple others.

I used to be really into woodworking. I gravitated toward rustic pieces because they left room for my mistakes. After all, I'm not exactly a detail-oriented guy. While working, I'd invite the guys I was discipling to join me. We'd talk about our families, our relationship with Jesus, fantasy football, and anything else that came up. It always turned into a fun time to connect and a moment to step back and admire what we'd created with our own hands. Discipleship requires intentional time to press in and talk, but it's also about creating touchpoints throughout the week. This wasn't our regular coffee shop meeting (we still had those). This was another opportunity to check in and do life together.

As I disciple my daughter, this concept has been pivotal. I've made it a point to invite Lilla to join me in whatever I'm doing. When I vacuum the floors, we crank up worship music, and she follows behind with our Swiffer mop. Does she do a great job as she dance-mops across the living room floor? Not really. It usually looks more like someone trying to mop while being chased by an alligator (she's a big fan of zigzag patterns). I often end up pausing my vacuuming to coach her on how to hold the mop, when to spray (and when not to—don't spray the cat!), and how to avoid missing spots. Last time, when she started to get discouraged, I put her on my shoulders and let her guide me while I finished the work. She giggled, while my back silently protested the whole ordeal. It's definitely more work for me to have her help! But it's also fun. She's not just learning how to mop the floor. We are spending intentional time together, maintaining our connection.

The current pulls us toward rushing to get things done, which often means we either handle it ourselves or decide our kids should figure it out alone and be more responsible. But if I'm going somewhere, I'm not going alone! This goes beyond giving my daughter responsibility and a sense of pride in her hard work. Deep down, our kids long to be pursued.

> **If I'm going somewhere, I'm not going alone!**

This has been God's heart from the beginning of creation. Jesus was called Emmanuel, God with us. Were there easier ways to glorify Himself? Probably. He could have made us perfect, God-worshiping robots who functioned without need, help, or stumbling blocks. But that was never His design for us. God made a people so free that they could choose to reject Him. His people became so lost in their own choices that they could not survive without someone stepping in to save them. He knew this in advance, and He chose it. As we stumble through life, He constantly and patiently stops the vacuum and helps us learn how to hold the mop. Our kids are made to deeply desire an active, intentional relationship with their parents. They want to go with you, but they'll slow you down along the way. I remember when I was a young child, walking two miles with my grandparents one morning. Toward the end of the trip, I was exhausted and struggling to keep up, so my grandfather, noticing my fatigue, pulled me along by the neck to get me to finish. But that's not the model we should follow. Bringing your child along with you will require slowing your pace, and your patience will undoubtedly be tested. You don't do it to finish quickly or achieve better results. You do it so they have someone beside them for the journey.

In Matthew 14, Jesus is with His disciples when a crowd of five thousand men gathered nearby. They had traveled from all over to hear the teachings of this man, who they heard was performing miracles. They came to witness firsthand the amazing things that had already reached their ears. After some time, the disciples approached Jesus with a very real problem.

There were simply too many people to feed, and they suggested it might be best to send them home so they could take care of themselves. Jesus listened to their concerns and responded, "You give them something to eat." Dumbfounded, the disciples were at a loss for what to do. Surely, the Son of God couldn't mean what He said. So they tried to clarify. "We only have two fish and five loaves of bread unless we buy more food from the market, but even then, the cost would be extreme." I imagine Jesus smiling at this point, much like I would when my daughter comes up with a solution that's just a little off the mark. "Have them sit down," Jesus replied. At this moment, Jesus could have solved the problem in any number of ways. He could have given them some manna, that heavenly bread that God provided to the Israelites during their time of wandering. He could have made quail appear as He had done before. He could have even brought Jacob back to life to serve some of his birthright stew. But instead, He blessed the bread and fish, then instructed His disciples to distribute it among the people. When everyone had been served, the disciples returned with more food than when they started!

God could have solved this problem on His own, but He didn't. Still, He played an essential role in the solution (without the miracle, there wouldn't have been enough food for the twelve). Even though Jesus was the key ingredient in this miracle, He included His disciples. He empowered them—those He was intentionally leading—to take part in the miracle. Jesus could have gone alone. It would have been easier, but He chose to invite them into the work. When we do this with our kids, it's not without risk. I'm still waiting for Lilla to drop a plate while helping with the dishes, just as Jesus doesn't have to wait long for us to mess things up. But a failure-free life is not the goal of discipleship. Your primary goal isn't to complete chores; it's to disciple your children to be sons and daughters of the King. There will be broken dishes along the way. Sometimes, you'll have to re-mop the whole house. It happens…and it's okay because we're in this together.

Over the past two years, I've picked up disc golf. It has the coolness factor of bowling, but with a better view. Even though it doesn't do much for my street cred, I absolutely love it. I've made it a point to invite my daughter to join me whenever possible. I've been disqualified from more than one tournament because she needed to use the bathroom mid-round. Having her with me hasn't helped my PDGA rating (yes, that's a thing) and certainly hasn't brought me any closer to a tournament win, but it's become a time I always look forward to. If you ask her right now, she'll also tell you she loves disc golf. But here's the thing: she doesn't. She has no idea how to play. The par scoring system isn't exactly 5-year-old-friendly. She has no clue how to play or what winning even looks like. All she knows is that disc golf means time with her Dad. She doesn't love disc golf. She loves me. And in her world, that's all that really matters.

I recently read that babies in orphanages don't cry. These tiny souls are often placed in overcrowded situations with staff who can't meet their needs, and as a result, they don't respond to a baby's cry. In that environment, an infant learns that crying won't change anything. Crying out will, at best, return an echo with no help to be found. Eventually, they stop. It's one of the saddest things I've ever heard, yet it's not an unfamiliar concept here in America. Sure, we've swapped orphanages for the foster care system, but the problem goes beyond that. Right now, we have kids in our homes who are desperate for their parents to include them. They want to grab your hand and know they're invited to walk by your side.

> **If you don't disciple your kids, someone else will.**

They need to feel that they aren't just an obstacle to your busy schedule, your need to make money, or your personal desires. Slowly, our children are learning that their cries to join in are futile, falling on deaf ears. They build walls against their parents, seeking others who will take them along instead. Unlike an infant, a child is capable of finding what they need elsewhere. Your kids were made to be discipled. If you don't disciple your kids, someone else will. Before you know it, pop culture will be guiding your kids. Television, social media, and the opinions of their friends will become the compass your kids rely on to guide them. Our voice grows smaller, while the noise around us gets louder. If we don't take them with us, someone else will.

Matt and Jess have spent considerable time developing a family strategy as they bring their three kids along with them. First, they asked themselves what they wanted their family to represent, and what their core values would be. Our church staff has core values that guide our hiring decisions. If a potential candidate is missing any of these values, they can't be hired. Similarly, Matt and Jess are determining the essential values that will shape their family into what God intended it to be. They want these core values instilled in their kids, and the best way to do that is to bring them along. One of their core values is being community builders. I've seen this firsthand. Wherever they go, they make it a point to create a biblical community. One example is their family dinners on their Sabbath, where they intentionally invite people from their community to join them. Jennie and I have been invited several times, and let me tell you, you're missing out. Jess's mom can cook! She trained as a chef in Europe, which I think is probably a big deal. Even years later, they're still hosting these community-building family dinners, but with one remarkable difference: their four-year-old son invites the guests. They've brought him along and involved him in the process. They've even taken this core value and considered how they'll engage their kids in the tradition at different stages. Eventually, their kids won't just send the invitations, they'll get to choose who to invite. It's a beautiful example of setting a family goal and intentionally bringing them along.

However, taking them along becomes even more challenging when we factor in our busy schedules. I imagine Jesus' days were filled with more campfires and longer walks. On the other hand, ours are filled with short commutes, long workdays, and constant busyness. I honestly can't remember the last time I asked someone how they were doing and didn't get the response, "Good, but busy." As our schedules fill up, the 'most important' relationships tend to get pushed out of sight and out of mind. Have you ever noticed that the times you're busiest are often when you spend the least amount of quality time with Jesus? I've fallen into the same pattern, busying Jesus right out of my schedule and then wondering why I feel so tired and burnt out. Oh yeah, the one who strengthens me is the guy I haven't seen in a week. Funny how that works.

This is our trap. We get so busy with things that don't matter that we end up offering our families the leftovers of what truly does. In Malachi, God's people did the same thing. They went to His temple and gave Him offerings that were just scraps. Instead of the best sheep, they offered blind or sick ones. They gave Him their leftovers, hoping it would be enough. God's response was blunt. "Oh, that one of you would shut the temple doors, so that you would not light useless fires on my altar! I am not pleased with you" (Malachi 1:10). He called their secondhand offerings a useless fire, and useless fires are the last thing your family needs. Your first ministry isn't your work, your church, or the evangelism poker game you host every Wednesday night. Your first ministry is your family. If your kids only get your leftovers, don't be surprised when they stop showing up to the table.

If your kids only get your leftovers, don't be surprised when they stop showing up to the table.

Our busyness often keeps us from giving our families everything we're meant to give. Actually, that's not quite right. It's not the busyness; it's our priorities (I know, I know…here we are again). Jesus wasn't without busyness. He lived in it. People were constantly coming to Him for help. But in the midst of all that, He never lost sight of the most important things. That's why He always found time to slip away and be with His Dad. And that's why He always returned to those twelve bumbling disciples, despite their endless confusion.

We're always going to be busy. I don't need to fill my schedule. It fills itself. Here's the solution: Get better at saying no. I'm serious. I learned early on that every time I say yes, I'm saying no to something else. I get it. This is tough. It's easy to be agreeable and become a "yes" person, but you weren't created to be a "yes" person. You were made to be a disciple-maker, which means you need to be willing to face uncomfortable situations. When I recognize that my "yes" means saying "no" somewhere else, I can count the cost and ensure the most important things are tied to my yes and the less important things aren't. We need to ensure our priorities are locked in and we're not giving our families and God the leftover scraps. One of the simplest ways to do this is by taking them with you. I want my daughter to be part of my schedule and know she's important and a priority.

One of the biggest challenges of busyness is that, as our children grow, we let their schedules drive ours. But what if we made a shift? As a student pastor, I've had countless parents tell me their child desperately needs biblical community and positive influences. They express frustration, saying they want their kids to be involved in our student ministry, but their child's baseball league takes up most weeknights and Sundays. I can't tell you how often I hear this same story. The solution is clear, yet we often overlook it. What's truly important? I've told parents that our Wednesday night ministry isn't the issue. If they need a ministry that fits better with their schedule, they should find one. But if community is truly vital, why do we let other activities push it out of our lives? I've seen many parents give in, resigning themselves to their current situation. I'm not anti-sports. I love sports, but we are laying the groundwork for what our kids will learn to prioritize. We need to make time for what matters most.

It's easy to claim that God is our top priority, but if we examine our bank accounts and schedules, our true idols are exposed. We are shaping these priorities in the hearts of our children. Once again, I'm not suggesting that student ministry is the solution. But I am saying that preparing your child's heart to walk with Jesus should always take precedence over the busyness that fills our lives.

Even if our schedules weren't the issue, many parents still struggle with involving their children in the most important aspects of life. Growing up, I was always told that our relationship with God was incredibly personal, so we didn't talk about Him much. It's remarkable how we can be so right and so wrong at the same time.

Our relationship with Jesus is meant to be deeply personal, but it was never meant to be private. If privacy were the goal, the book of Acts would have looked very different. Our faith is something we are meant to share with our children so they can learn and grow from it. I'm not just talking about a Bible study or quiet time together. I'm saying that my faith and walk with Jesus should be so ingrained in my heart that it overflows into everything else. We naturally talk about the things we love most, and Jesus should be at the center of it all.

I've heard parents push back on this idea, saying they don't want to choose God for their kids. "I want them to figure it out for themselves," they argue. But let's take a closer look at that logic. Do we apply the same hands-off approach when teaching our kids to drive? Absolutely not. We don't just hand them the keys and hope they figure it out. Instead, we guide them every step of the way—coaching them to adjust their mirrors, come to a complete stop at signs, and use their turn signals correctly. We don't want them to navigate the road alone; we want to ensure they get it right.

Yet, we often take a different approach to faith. Why? Because we tend to place greater emphasis on the physical than the spiritual. Maybe it's because the physical feels more tangible, or maybe it's simply that we're more comfortable teaching driving skills than sharing the Gospel.

> **Our relationship with Jesus is meant to be deeply personal, but it was never meant to be private.**

But if Jesus truly is who He says He is, then how much more important is your child's faith? The truth is: You can't choose God for your kids, but you can guide them toward making the right choice—just like you would with anything else that truly matters. As parents, it's our responsibility to invite our kids into our daily time with Jesus because parenting against the current keeps eternity in focus. As parents, it's our responsibility to invite our kids into our daily time with Jesus because parenting against the current keeps eternity in focus.

I try to spend time with Jesus in the Word every day. I wish I could say I always do, but if I'm being honest, Jesus never misses a meeting, but sometimes I do. However, there is one day I never miss. It's one I've come to look forward to each week. As you know, my wife teaches kindergarten, and our daughter is also in kindergarten. Most days, Lilla rides to school with Jennie, except on Fridays. I have Fridays off, so I wake up early to get Lilla ready for school. Before I drop her off, we stop at the local coffee shop. I order coffee, she orders a blueberry muffin, and we sit down with Jesus. She's five, so our Jesus time looks a bit different than my solo time with Him. It's a precious time for the three of us to connect. We pray, read a short story from her kids' Bible, and then she opens her journal to draw a picture of what she heard. Afterward, I ask, "What do you think God is telling you?" She'll choose a simple phrase like, "I can trust God" or "Jesus loves big." She writes the phrase next to her picture (with a little help on the spelling). I'll date it and write the Bible reference at the top, then send a photo to Mom to see if she can guess which story we read. I'm not sure if Jennie needs to brush up on her Bible stories or if Lilla inherited my poor artistic abilities (probably the latter), but Jennie usually doesn't guess correctly. I'm not sure if we're winning Bible Pictionary, but we're definitely playing. Afterward, we grab coffee for some of Jennie's coworkers, hit the road, and talk about what God spoke to us as we pull into the school parking lot. The crazy thing is, I'm not sure who looks forward to our discipleship time more. Every Friday, I give up a little sleep to remind my daughter whose she is. We're not having theological debates. She's five. I don't need to have all the answers. I just need to love Jesus and push against the current as I take her with me.

Reflection

1. How is your connection with your child?
a. Take a moment to assess your connection with your child honestly. This isn't about what you wish was true but understanding where you stand. Honesty is vital for meaningful growth.

2. What do you need to allow Jesus to change in your heart towards your child?

3. How can you and your spouse intentionally meet your child/children where they are?
a. Who have you told your child that he/she is by your words and actions? Is that consistent with who Jesus created them to be?

4. Look at your schedule. What activities are you already doing that you can invite your child or children to?
a. What are your reservations, and should they stop you? Remember that the goal isn't speed or excellence. It is about growing a deeper connection.

Challenge

Discover something your child loves and make an intentional effort to join them in it. Do they love sports? Play catch with them. Is she all about princesses? Get dressed up and take her on a special outing. This isn't about making them do what you love but about stepping into their world to build a deeper connection. Discover what they love, join them there, and make it a regular part of your time together.

Family Trip

Remember MapQuest? It was this groundbreaking technology that gave you directions to almost any destination. You'd fire up your computer, connect to the internet (while praying no one called to interrupt your dial-up), and print out the step-by-step instructions. Then, you'd tear off the perforated edges of the paper (if you know, you know) and hit the road, squinting at your printout while driving. Whenever my family went on a big road trip, we relied on MapQuest, or an actual map, to make sure we reached our destination. Things haven't changed much, except for the tech. I even have a buddy who's lived in Houston for four years and still uses his phone to navigate nearby places. I'm not kidding. He probably uses it to find the gas station across the street.

Clear directions are essential for reaching any destination. Yet many parents lack a parenting roadmap and a clearly defined end goal. Every successful journey requires both.

Those who walk in darkness can't see what they stumble over (paraphrasing Proverbs 4:19). But [God's] word is a lamp for my feet, a light on my path. While the Bible isn't a map in the traditional sense, it's an essential tool for navigating life's complexities. It illuminates our path and helps us identify a biblical destination to guide our parenting.

For the sake of discussion, let's assume we've all agreed on the following destination.

That our kids: Love God (Matthew 22:37), love others (Matthew 22:39), and enjoy us (Proverbs 17:6).

Reaching the destination will be a lifelong process. But a destination this important is worth the gas.

Once we have a biblical destination and a roadmap, we gain a lens through which to filter decisions as we actively work against the current. With a clear destination, we can evaluate our direction and plan our stops along the way. For instance, traveling from Houston to Miami, you wouldn't detour to the Space Needle—it's completely out of the way! Every pitstop, gas station, diner, and bathroom break should move you one step closer to your target and further against the current.

To be clear, Jesus can use nearly any activity to draw us closer to Himself. Your child's soccer practice could be a meaningful pitstop. A piano recital could serve as a checkpoint as you go. It could be, but it's up to you to evaluate it and determine if it truly is. Too often, we fill our schedules without considering the impact these activities have on the journey.

Personally, sports have been a great space for me to deepen my love for Jesus. I've always enjoyed competition, and I've had the privilege of reminding others that while I may love to win, it's not the ultimate reason I'm there. That said, I've also had moments when competition consumed me and created division in relationships. In those times, I had to decide whether to invite Jesus into that activity or to cut it out of my life altogether (looking at you, fantasy football).

Ultimately, it's less about what your children are doing and more about asking whether those things are helping them move closer to the target.

The most important destination our children can reach is a deep love for Christ, but traffic flow around us often heads in the opposite direction. You're in the driver's seat with your MapQuest directions. As you travel, take in the views, navigate the oncoming traffic, and cherish the journey. It's a beautiful scene, made even sweeter by those traveling with you. As you pass each exit, don't be tempted to veer off course. Stay steady and focused on the destination to which you've been called.

How to Travel

In college, I got my first car—or, more accurately, my parents bought it. We agreed on a loose repayment plan, though I had no real concept of what that meant. I had no clue what I was looking for as I browsed car lots. My only goal was to drive somewhere, and I didn't care much about the kind of vehicle that would take me there. Ultimately, I settled on a $2,000 1999 manual Ford Escort.

Excited to test my new wheels, I convinced my little brother to join me on an impromptu road trip to Orlando. We had a blast during the first part of the drive, but about 2.5 hours in, the car started slowing down. Then, it just stopped. After a short wait, I managed to get it running again, only for it to sputter out thirty minutes later.

Frustrated but determined, I visited multiple auto shops to diagnose the issue. None of them could pinpoint the problem, but I had my theory: the car just got tired. Whenever she needed a break, she'd stop until she regained the energy to keep going.

Eventually, I gave up on Orlando and headed home. What should have been a 2.5-hour trip turned into a two-day ordeal, complete with frequent breakdowns and, ultimately, a tow for the last 100 miles. I had a car, a destination, and all the motivation in the world, but I never actually made it.

Learning to read a map and define a destination are just parts of a much larger puzzle. We also need to understand how we'll get there. Even with the best-planned trip and a clear goal, you'll never make it if you choose the wrong vehicle.

During my time in the Army, I worked on tanks. It was common for me to hop inside one of those behemoths and tinker around. I thought they were incredibly cool and even dreamed of taking one for a spin. But here's the thing: I never would've attempted to take it to Hawaii even if I could've driven that tank. Why? Because the Army is still working on waterproofing their Abrams tanks. It wouldn't make sense and certainly wouldn't get me where I needed to go.

Fear tactics, anger, manipulation, and displays of power are common vehicles parents use to maintain control. And, to a degree, they work. You have successfully found a way to temporarily ensure that your child is quiet in the back seat, and if that is your destination, then keep driving that tank. Sometimes, we opt for a quieter route in our quest for peace, choosing passivity to create an illusion of harmony. If that sounds familiar, you would've loved my Ford Escort. But none of these vehicles will ever take you to the biblical destination God's Word calls us to as parents and disciples. When it comes to parenting, love is the only vehicle that will truly get us there.

It seems like common sense, but drift is sneaky like that. As parents, we can get so focused on reaching our destination that our vehicle shifts into anger, frustration, or an overpowering drive to keep going. It's like when your child suddenly has to pee just thirty minutes into your vacation, and you strategically "miss" the next six exits. You're frustrated! They should have gone before you left; even if they had, they shouldn't have consumed so many Capri Suns. That liquid joy was supposed to last all day! They're slowing you down, and you have places to go. In that moment, your vehicle becomes something other than what it was meant to be. Love is always moving against the current. It's an intentional choice that requires effort and endurance.

When Lilla was learning to swim, she had one big fear: water slides. She wanted to go down them and knew I wanted her to enjoy them too, but she was so scared that she wouldn't even approach the stairs. I love watching my girl conquer her fears, so I poured a lot of effort into helping her that day. We spent time talking through it. Then, we'd go up the stairs and watch other kids slide down. An hour later, Lilla had made incredible progress. We even got to the point where she would sit on the edge of the slide. But even then, she wouldn't take the plunge. She had come so far that day, but I kept pushing her to be brave until she finally broke down. That's when Jennie (who had been gently hinting at this for a while) asked me why I couldn't celebrate the small wins.

That was a sobering moment for me because, in an instant, it became clear that not only had my vehicle changed, but so had my destination. This wasn't about her loving God or others, or enjoying a day at the pool with her parents. We had one destination in mind, and it looked like the bottom of that slide. Was my heart evil and corrupt?

No, but drift often wears camouflage. It's a subtle shift that happens without us even noticing. My daughter was tired, done, and had already conquered mountains in her battle against fear. Love should have looked like a parade. But instead, I traded love for a tank and became upset when it started to leak. I'm grateful that my wife is always willing to help me identify my drift and hold me steady as I regain my footing.

> **Drift often wears camouflage. It's a subtle shift that happens without us even noticing.**

If the destination of your parenting is obedience, there are many vehicles to choose from. You can easily raise your voice, threaten, or scare them so they know you're powerful and in control with phrases like, "Don't make me pull this car over!" You'll reach your destination, and they'll be quiet and obedient along the way. But be aware. They're just as likely to roll out in their own armored vehicle, ready to face your tank head-on with defiance and rebellion. Without a doubt, you'll get somewhere. But inferior vehicles lead to inferior destinations. The goal is a relationship—with God, others, and you. A strong relationship with your child will help them build a strong, independent relationship with God; love is the only vehicle built to make the distance.

Why have you placed your faith in Jesus? Is it because you're afraid of Him? Because you feel manipulated by Him? Is it out of guilt? If that's the case, I think we are following a different person. I'm not minimizing God's wrath, which is a very real part of His character, nor am I saying there isn't a time for discipline and consequences. I'm simply asserting that we shouldn't be swapping cars as we go. If you are angry, let it be anger driven by love. Love is what gives everything we do value (1 Corinthians 13). Romans 2:4 says, "God's kindness (not strength, not power, not anger) is intended to lead you to repentance." Repentance is when we experience conviction over our brokenness and choose to turn from it. We literally turn against the current and begin walking in the opposite direction. Why? Is it because we're afraid of what He will do if we don't? No! It's His kindness, His love, and His grace that transform us.

In Matthew 26, Jesus exemplifies this through His actions. By this point, He had told His disciples that He was about to be killed. In response, He gathered them together and spent the night in prayer with His Father.

[47] While he was still speaking, Judas, one of the Twelve, arrived. With him was a large crowd armed with swords and clubs, sent from the chief priests and the elders of the people. [48] Now the betrayer had arranged a signal with them: "The one I kiss is the man; arrest him." [49] Going at once to Jesus, Judas said, "Greetings, Rabbi!" and kissed him. [50] Jesus replied, "Do what you came for, friend."

The vehicles are chosen. The soldiers and priests are ready for a fight, armed with their Humvees and anything else needed to throw down. Judas chose deception as his vehicle—a tactic often leveraged by parents. As for Jesus, at this point, it's unclear what He's going to pull out of the garage.

Then the men stepped forward, seized Jesus, and arrested him. [51] With that, one of Jesus' companions reached for his sword, drew it out, and struck the servant of the high priest, cutting off his ear.

I'm not sure what kind of wonky sword swing it takes to cut off an ear and nothing else, but Peter (identified in other Gospels as our master swordsman) boldly declares, "Let me show you how I travel!" It's so easy to watch how others get around and follow their lead. When your kids get rude, how do you respond? It's tempting to get rude right back. They yell, and we yell louder. We want to be in charge, but we often let them choose the vehicle. Jesus, however, doesn't do that.

[52] *"Put your sword back in its place," Jesus said to him, "for all who draw the sword will die by the sword.* [53] *Do you think I cannot call on my Father, and he will at once put at my disposal more than twelve legions of angels?*

Jesus is clear. He tells Peter, "If you're going to ride with Me, you need to ride like Me." He makes it plain to the soldiers: if His goal were to prove who was in charge, they'd already be dust. He has everything He needs. You've got Humvees? He's got legions of angels! They never stood a chance. And yet.

Jesus chose a different destination—and with it, a different vehicle.

[51] But Jesus answered, *"No more of this!"* And he touched the man's ear and healed him. (Luke 22:51)

Jesus had access to every car in the dealership but refused to let the vehicles of others dictate His ride. While others rode for war, Jesus chose a different path. He doesn't follow currents. His destination for us has always been about teaching us to love Him, and that starts with Him first loving us (1 John 4:19).

Before we dive into strategies and methods, it's crucial to know how we travel. Love must be the driving force behind everything we do. It's this love that often gives you the strength to push against the current when it urges you to surrender and drift away. Your strengths, skills, job title, or salary don't determine your success as a parent. Love is the vehicle; without it, you're left with a broken-down car that never makes it to Orlando.

Mile Markers

We face a familiar challenge in student ministry: high school students often seem much more mature than middle schoolers. I know—crazy, right? This ministerial "phenomenon" has left many leaders puzzled as they watch senior groups "thrive" while struggling to convince their sixth-grade boys to stop burping the alphabet during small group. As amusing as this may sound, it's a genuine struggle for many middle school leaders who sacrificially serve in the beautiful chaos of youth ministry. Watching other groups succeed, they can quickly feel defeated, discouraged, and disheartened.

Parents, you know the feeling. As proud as you are of your child, it's easy to fall into the dangerous trap of comparing their behavior, maturity, intelligence, and athleticism to their siblings or other people's kids. We scroll through Instagram, seeing families who never seem to disagree, are always reading the Bible, and appear to have it all together. And we wonder: What's wrong with me? What's wrong with my spouse? What's wrong with our kids? Why aren't we as Instagram-happy as all those families we see online?

First off, stop trusting the highlight reels. No parent intentionally strives to raise their child and doesn't struggle at some point. Didn't you read the first chapter? It's all about sacrifice and pushing against a current that just won't quit. We're in it for the long haul, creating disciples who love and live like Him. It's a very challenging process, which means we need to celebrate our milestones along the way.

If you're on a long trip, you probably don't measure your victories by the final destination—not right away, anyway. Instead, you focus on mile markers that show your progress or perhaps the next lunch stop. As we travel, we shorten the distance between us and the destination because, honestly, the end goal can feel too far away. The truth is, my middle school leaders are doing an incredible job. I watch them pour into our students, loving them in the midst of the chaos. These volunteers are some of the fiercest Kingdom warriors I know, and they need mile markers to remind them that they're winning. I don't want them to see our senior students hosting quiet time takeovers at the local coffee shop and feel discouraged that their own students—who can't even drive yet—aren't doing the same. That's not an appropriate mile marker based on their students' maturity. We need victories that match where our kids are.

Guard your heart. Your child was not created or designed to be like someone else's. Whether you feel like you're failing or your pride is seeking validation, there's no good reason to compare your child to others. Every child is unique and has their own path to follow as they become who they were created to be. Your job is not to compare paths; it's to help them reach their destination and enjoy the journey. As parents, we all love celebrating the home runs our kids hit. But what about the more subtle victories—the ones that don't make the highlight reel? Like when your daughter strikes out but, instead of throwing her helmet, she lifts her chin and cheers for the next batter. Or when school feels like an uphill battle, yet your son keeps giving it his all, even if the test scores don't reflect his effort. It's not about the victory you had in mind. It's about recognizing and celebrating every step, even the unexpected ones, that bring them closer to Jesus. Small wins are still wins. Celebrate the mile markers. We don't need more spiritual infants in adult bodies. Remember, every child develops at their own pace. These milestones serve as guides, not rules, as you move your family closer and closer to maturity.

> **Small wins are still wins. Celebrate the mile markers.**

Mile markers by age

Maturity varies from child to child, and these ages are only guidelines. Don't feel bad if you need to adjust these for your child. Traveling is never about where you are, but about where you're headed.

0-24 Months Old

Your child knows that they are loved and safe with you. This is your time to show them that you are a safe place to run to and that your arms are ready to hold them. At this age, they are watching you. You are the earthly reflection of a heavenly parent, and it's your responsibility to do your best to communicate love and trust.

This life stage is largely for the parent. You are learning, growing, and maturing. You're beginning to realize just how sacrificial parenting can be. Use this time intentionally and strategically. A big part of parenting is using the ordinary to communicate the divine. Although they are little, it's not too early to teach them about God's love for them. What if, every night before bed, you shared the Gospel with your child through a simple toy? It might feel jumbled in the first few weeks, but after a few months, you'll start seeking out the most challenging things in the room to share the gospel through. A lamp? *Too easy.* How about a didgeridoo? It will become a game for you as you grow more skilled in sharing the Gospel. You have two years to fumble through this process while growing in your ability to share God's truth.

There will come a day when your child will need to hear the truth about Jesus from you. Use these years so you will be equipped for those later conversations. This has been a game-changer for Matt and his wife, Jess. They made it a point to do this with each of their kids during their first year. It's so easy to overcomplicate the Gospel, but these moments helped them—and can help us—be prepared for future conversations.

2-5 Years Old

At this stage, your child knows about Jesus. They've seen your personal relationship with Him in action and are beginning to ask questions. They enjoy reading their children's Bible, can retell some of their favorite stories, and might even have a favorite character. Lilla's favorite is Samson. I'm still trying to disciple that one out of her! You're growing in understanding, too! It's amazing how teaching Scripture (even with a kid's Bible) will grow your own knowledge of who God is.

Your child might start asking you questions you don't know how to answer. That's amazing! Celebrate their curiosity and use those moments to search for answers together. These are the years when they learn about God's character and begin to understand how to live it out. They're also starting to grasp how to regulate their emotions and practice loving others well. They're learning what it means to lose graciously, and you're there to remind them of the real wins in life.

Fill your home with worship music. Chances are, your child loves to sing and dance, so give them music that feeds their spirit and fills their heart with joy. Worship with them, sing with them, and dance with them!

Not a great singer? Me neither. But you know who doesn't notice or care? Your kids! Besides, David reminds us in Psalms 100:1 to make a joyful noise unto the Lord. Your kids don't care about your vocal technique. To them, you're a Christian Bruno Mars, ready to rock out for Jesus—and the best part is, they're ready to rock out too. Long before your kids start memorizing Bible verses, they'll memorize songs. Give them something meaningful to sing about, and fill your home with melodies that glorify God. You'll be amazed at how many songs they'll know just because your house is painted with worship.

6-14 Years Old

This is the sweet spot. During this stage, many kids begin a genuine, personal relationship with Jesus. According to a study by the National Association of Evangelicals, 63% of Christians accept Jesus between ages 4 and 14.[2] This makes these years a pivotal time in their faith journey.

---

[2] National Association of Evangelicals, "Most Evangelicals Became Christians Before Age 14," *NAE News*, March 2015, https://www.nae.net/most-evangelicals-became-christians-before-age-14.

Your child is starting to own their faith, even though self-discipline and consistency may still be developing. They are beginning to take responsibility for their walk with Jesus. At this age, your child might be baptized and can start serving others. While their focus might not yet entirely shift to giving back, they are capable of helping in meaningful ways. Your child might also begin having their own devotional or quiet times with you or on their own, and you may start to see the fruit of their faith. Celebrate these milestones and encourage them as they take steps forward in their relationship with Jesus.

This is your opportunity to truly and intentionally disciple your child. While you've been discipling them all along, now is the time to shift into a new gear. Become an expert in asking meaningful questions. Just as you are a student of your spouse, become a student of your children. Learn about their hearts, passions, and challenges. Your child will likely have many questions about navigating situations or understanding theology. When they come to you, start by asking what they think. This approach helps them work toward discovering the truth rather than simply receiving it from you. Of course, this doesn't mean you shouldn't step in and provide guidance—especially if their answer is off track. Instead, it means encouraging them to think critically and wrestle with the questions. The better your questions, the clearer a picture you'll have of who your child is and who they are becoming.

15+ Years Old

At this stage, your child can become a champion of their own faith, often sharing it with others. Some of the boldest evangelists I know are still teenagers—fearless and eager to spread the Good News with abandon. At this age, they might lead others to Jesus, baptize friends, serve together, and dive deep into a biblical community. Parents may feel like their kids are pulling away, but it's important to remember that this is a victory. A crucial part of discipleship is sending them out.

But as they step out in faith, it may not always look the way we expected. As parents, we pray for our children to develop their own relationship with Jesus—to hear His voice and follow His leading. Yet sometimes, His direction for their lives won't align with the plans we envisioned for them. They may make decisions—like stopping a sport, choosing a college, or pursuing a calling—that stretch our trust in God's work in their lives. This is where our role shifts from directing to supporting, trusting that the same God who has led us is now leading them, even in ways He may not have revealed to us.

At this stage, your kids might be more interested in spending time with their friends than with you, but they still need a place to gather. Be that house. Create an environment where your kids want their friends to come over. Make sure those friends feel welcomed and part of the family. When your home becomes the hub, you are better equipped to influence culture as your child begins to take independent steps.

Remember, these phases are the target. Don't get upset or discouraged if your family isn't there yet. These ages are simply guidelines—every situation and every child is different. Don't let it dishearten you if your child isn't meeting the milestones tied to a specific age. Your role is to plant seeds and water the crop, but God makes things grow. These mile markers are designed to help you identify and correct any drift that may be occurring. Drift is natural and to be expected, but that's not a reason to stay off course. Take a moment to pray intentionally for your child as they take the next steps toward maturity. Seriously. Stop right now, put the book down, and pray for your kids. Think about where they are and what they need to take the next step. If your child hasn't chosen to follow Jesus yet, pray that they will come to know Him early in life and follow Him all their days. Pray for wisdom as you become a student of your child. Pray for open doors that lead to deeper connections. Perhaps reading through these stages brought up feelings of shame or guilt about where your kids are. The devil is real. He is a liar, a thief, and a murderer. He delights in leaving you with lies of guilt and shame, but these are not the voice or heart of our Heavenly Father.

Ask God to replace those lies with truth. Ask Him for encouragement and a community to support you on this journey. You are not in a race with other parents. You are simply celebrating your family's own mile markers as you work toward the destination.

Pull the Car Over

Sometimes, the strongest current I battle is my own momentum. When I'm focused on reaching a destination, I want nothing more than to get there, leaving no room for interruptions or distractions. Yet, in the real world, parenting carries the tagline: Expect constant interruptions. Most of us can't even flush the toilet before being called to handle something, and if you're like me, that's undeniably frustrating. But what if we reframed interruptions from obstacles to opportunities?

Lilla and I drove to a friend's house for dinner one evening. We needed to stop by the grocery store to pick up a few things so we wouldn't arrive empty-handed. It was close to Christmas, and our church had planned a special choir performance for the holiday service. I was excited that my wife and daughter had signed up to sing. I rarely get to sit in the seats while they're on stage, and I couldn't have been more excited. Lilla and I had been working to find opportunities for her to be brave, and singing in front of a crowd was the perfect challenge. During the car ride to the store, we practiced the song together. But no matter how much I encouraged her, she barely sang above a whisper.

When we got to the store, I decided to make it a game—who could sing the loudest in front of total strangers? Yes… I'm that guy.

Pro tip: One of the simplest ways to show love is to care more about the person you're with than how silly you might look to others. Or at least, that's my excuse for dancing and singing at the top of my lungs through our local grocery store. It was a blast, and she completely got into it.

As we got back to the car, even though we were running late, I felt a deep sense of connection between us. That's when Lilla began asking questions about the song we had sung and about Jesus. She was determined to understand how she could choose to follow Him.

For the next 15 minutes, we talked about Jesus and why we so desperately need Him. It wasn't the first time we'd had this conversation, but this time felt different. Every other time, she would eventually get distracted or zone out, and I wouldn't push. Following Jesus needed to be her decision, something she chose when her heart was truly ready. But now, as she asked her questions and I asked some back, she was fully engaged. Every word was sincere, a yearning to truly know Him. We were already late for a dinner I had been looking forward to, but I felt a tug on my heart: I needed to stop the car and embrace this interruption.

> **One of the simplest ways to show love is to care more about the person you're with than how silly you might look to others.**

Jesus wasn't a stranger to interruptions. In Luke 8, He was on His way to save a young girl who was gravely ill. This girl was dying, and Jesus was walking with her father, Jairus, to heal her. But along the way, a woman suffering from a bleeding illness for twelve years reached out in faith and touched His cloak. She was instantly healed. And what did Jesus do? He stopped. YES, STOPPED. Picture it: a dying girl, a desperate father, and a healed woman. Yet Jesus decided it was the perfect moment to pause and have a conversation. Can you imagine being Jairus in that situation? I'd be losing my mind. *We have places to be! My daughter is dying! This woman is already healed—and even if she wasn't, her need doesn't seem as urgent. Jesus! Let's get back on the road!*

Even when they feel righteous and good, my own momentum and desires can leave me pressing forward, unwilling to be interrupted. The disciples experienced the same mindset when Jesus suddenly asked, "*Who touched me?*" Confused, they shrugged and pointed out that the crowd was pressing in from all sides. Everyone was touching Him!

But Jesus stopped. He took the time to speak with the woman He had just healed. For twelve long years, she had been labeled unclean. Society cast her aside as an outcast, and she lost everything she owned trying to find a cure. Jesus had already healed her body, but He stopped to heal her heart.

He wanted her to know she was loved and never abandoned. His words were even more powerful than physical healing: "*Daughter, your faith has made you well. Go in peace.*" At that moment, Jesus reminded her of who she truly was. He called her Daughter and restored her heart, even while Jairus' daughter lay dying.

As Jesus continued walking with Jairus, devastating news arrived: Jairus' daughter had died. This is the moment when our impatience screams that interruptions are obstacles meant to be bulldozed. We want to plow through them, refusing to slow down.

But here's the truth: Interruptions only become obstacles when the destination matters more than the people traveling with us. So, what about Jairus? What about his daughter? I'm glad you asked. When the news reached them, Jesus reassured Jairus, telling him to return home. His daughter had been healed.

> **Interruptions only become obstacles when the destination matters more than the people traveling with us.**

It's not that the destination wasn't important. It was. But it wasn't more important than taking the time to pull over.

As I worked on this chapter, I suddenly heard our daughter shout from upstairs. She had broken her wooden dollhouse and was really sorry. My first response? Honestly, I was annoyed. I didn't want to stop writing. It felt like such a silly interruption.

But don't worry. I checked my heart, told Jairus to hold tight, and headed upstairs to help her figure it out. After her rest time, she's going to learn about clamps and liquid nails as we tackle a dollhouse renovation together. Interruptions are part of parenting. We know this, but let's be honest: we hate pulling over. Slowing down feels inconvenient, and the current of our own momentum can be hard to resist. What about you? What are the little interruptions in your life you see as obstacles rather than opportunities? Are there specific areas where you struggle more than others? Here's a glimpse of the interruptions I've faced in just the last few hours:

- Where I'm headed: Writing a chapter on interruptions.
Interruption: Dollhouse's roof snapped off.
What I wanted to do: Ignore the irony and keep writing.

- Where I'm headed: Preparing the nursery for the baby.
Interruption: "Dad, I want to learn how to tie my shoes."
What I wanted to do: Freeze. If I don't move, maybe she won't see me.

- Where I'm headed- SLEEEEPPPPP.
Interruption: "Good morning, Daddy!"
What I wanted to do: Hibernate.

Interruptions are inevitable in parenting, but that doesn't mean you need to pull the car over for every single one. The point isn't that your kids dictate when you press the gas or hit the brake, but neither should your rush to get somewhere.

We need to stop driving as if our brake lines are cut while still recognizing the importance of healthy boundaries. If I'm in the middle of a conversation and my daughter needs something, I often ask her to wait. She knows I'll prioritize her when the time is right. I share this because there is a difference between welcoming interruptions and being owned by them. The truth is interruptions are opportunities. They're moments to remind our kids that they are seen, valued, and loved.

Even though we were running late for dinner, Lilla wanted to know more about following Jesus. I set aside my desire to get where I was going, pushed back against the pull of my own momentum, and pulled the car over.

I asked her if it was okay for me to hop into the back seat. Her response still makes me smile. "Sure! It looks so different back here." She cracks me up. We talked about sin and why we need Jesus. I asked her why she wanted to follow Him, and I listened as she answered with such intentionality and sincerity. Then, with a heart full of conviction, she told me she wanted to place her faith in Jesus. So, in the back of a random Cracker Barrel parking lot, my daughter began her relationship with Jesus. It's a memory I will cherish forever.

Don't get so caught up in what you're doing that you miss the chance to pull the car over. Don't allow your inertia to make slowing down the last thing you want to do. It can seem like an interruption to a bigger plan. But intentional parenting is often about embracing those interruptions, using them as moments to remind our kids who they are.

I Spy

What's traveling without some form of entertainment? If you've ever been on a road trip, chances are you've played I Spy. I have to be honest with you. After making it this far, I owe you that much. I despise this game. Finding things has never been my strength. Every Easter, my parents hid our baskets, apparently a weird tradition, according to my wife, and I always struggled to find mine, even when it was in plain sight. Then my mom would casually point to the counter, and there it would be, completely out in the open, zero camouflage. Jennie jokes that I need to "look with my eyes," whatever that means. Despite my dislike of the game (and, let's be honest, my complete inability to play it well), it's a traveling staple for kids everywhere. If you're unfamiliar, here's how it works: you pick something and then give clues for others to find it, too! I know, groundbreaking. But honestly, this game provides a pretty clear picture of what it looks like for Jennie and me to disciple our daughter on a regular basis.

As we journey together, take a moment to look out the window. The entirety of creation—every mountain, valley, person, and animal—points to the Creator. His fingerprints are everywhere. He's had His hand in creating everything under the moon, and everything beyond it, for that matter. In fact, He made the moon too. His fingerprints are all around us. They're not hard to find if you simply look with your eyes.

In Deuteronomy 6, Moses speaks this message from the Lord.

Hear, O Israel: The Lord our God, the Lord is one. Love the Lord your God with all your heart and with all your soul and with all your strength. These commandments that I give you today are to be on your hearts. Impress them on your children. Talk about them when you sit at home and when you walk along the road, when you lie down and when you get up. Tie them as symbols on your hands and bind them on your foreheads. Write them on the doorframes of your houses and on your gates.

If you've ever wondered if Moses dabbled in the occasional game of spiritual I Spy, the answer is yes. Moses is telling us that as parents, we're called to love God with everything we have and then share that love with the ones we love most. Are you walking? Find Him. Are you sitting? Find Him. We're meant to talk about the incredible God we serve and seek Him in the simple, everyday moments of life.

The best part is you don't need to be a scholar to play. You just need to look with your eyes! We've made it a tradition every night at dinner. I used to ask everyone at the table where they saw Jesus that day. Recently, though, Lilla "fired" me from this role, and now she asks the question. We've done this with just the three of us, and we've done it with guests in our home. It's a dining requirement. If you're riding with us, you're playing the game. Today, Lilla shared that she saw Jesus when He helped her be brave at school. I love that. Courage is something she's working hard to grow in, and I love that she recognized how Jesus helped her find it today. Every moment is a chance to find Jesus and share His truth.

The other day, I learned that my team, the Miami Dolphins, had cheated and lost several draft picks because of it. When I shared this with our five-year-old, she was confused. She couldn't understand why someone would want to cheat. I explained that sometimes people want to win more than they want to do what's right. "Why?" she asked. And just like that, we were no longer talking about a silly game or the mistakes of my favorite team. We were talking about sin and the role of the Holy Spirit. We discussed how sin works and how easy it is to follow its voice. I explained that we need to learn to listen to the Spirit of God because He will never lead us astray. This conversation wasn't about football or the mistakes of the team leaders. I don't know their story or their reasons, and that's not what mattered. This became an opportunity to share God's truth with my little girl. I wanted her to understand that He gave us the Holy Spirit to help us do what's right, even when our flesh wants something different. We could have been talking football, but instead, we were playing I Spy.

This brings us back to where we started. As parents, we cannot afford to be biblically illiterate. I'm not saying to go to seminary. I'm saying that we have a responsibility to understand the key themes of the Bible and the nature of God's character. When we grasp these truths, we'll be able to spot them in everyday life and point them out to the ones we love. As a helpful resource, a list of key themes and biblical references can be found in the resources section at the back of this book.

Every conversation is a chance to point our children toward God, equipping them to recognize His presence and give Him glory. As we recognize God's fingerprints in our lives and share them with our kids, we equip them to discover His presence for themselves. As they begin to see Him, they grow to love Him, and the more they love Him, the more they'll see Him.

Kids and Maps

I have a random yet vivid memory from Kindergarten. I was walking down the hallway of my school. As I walked, it hit me. I was already five years old, and in just thirteen years, I would be sent off to college, away from home, and my parents wouldn't be nearby. I've never been someone who gets easily anxious. Jennie jokes that I don't even know how to feel nervous. But in that moment, I felt a deep anxiety. Even at 5, I was wise enough to know I wasn't ready for what was coming, and the thought of leaving home terrified me.

HOW WAS I GOING TO SURVIVE?!

As parents, it's easy to recognize that we're navigating uncharted territory, trying to figure things out as we go. Every stage is new and unpredictable, and we don't always know how to get where we're headed. But we often forget that our kids are even more lost than we are. At least we have the advantage of knowing the world around us, some basic truths, and our own childhood experiences to guide us. Our kids have none of that. They haven't been given a map, and even if they had, they wouldn't know how to read it. They look out the window with no idea where they are or where they're going. In that hallway, kindergarten Josh had a moment of clarity: I was out of my depth. I didn't know how to read the map and needed someone to teach me.

Here's the tough part: every age is different. A big part of the journey is using your time to equip your child to actively participate. When a child is born, they ride in a car seat. Eventually, they graduate to a regular seat, but not the front. Fast forward, and they're in the passenger seat, still unable to drive. Then comes the permit, and finally, they're ready to hit the road on their own. We aren't just driving to a destination. We're growing and teaching along the way.

One of the ways we do this in our home is through anchor statements. Kids are eager to learn but need guidance tailored to their spiritual and developmental stage. Anchor statements work well for all ages, but we'll focus on ages 1-8. During this time, kids begin to figure out who they are, and simple phrases and definitions can help them learn how to read the map. We started by having our daughter repeat the phrase, but now we ask her what the word means or start the phrase and let her finish it. Teaching anchor statements is like handing your child a piece of the map they'll need to navigate life. Here are some examples we use in our home.

It's okay to be mad, but it's not okay to be mean. We don't want our child to become a professional people-pleaser, wearing a mask and hiding her feelings because she believes they can't be expressed or handled by others. Anger itself is not a sin, but what we do with it can be. We want our kids to understand that it's okay to feel anger, but they are still responsible for how they manage it and what actions they take because of it. Rather than labeling anger as bad, we teach them how to manage it constructively.

Patient means okay with waiting. When you're in line and your child is antsy, it's easy to say, "Hey, be patient!" But do they understand what it really means and why it's important? Providing opportunities for kids to practice patience is invaluable. It helps them understand that they aren't the center of the universe and teaches them how to be okay with a little boredom.

I will obey, the first time, all the way, without complaining. This is a great phrase we borrowed from some people in our community. Each section is a prompt for your child to repeat. In this phrase, you are teaching your child both how to win and how to be respectful. But let's be clear. The *why* behind it is crucial. The goal of parenting is not simply obedience. The goal is love. As it says in 1 John, "Love for God is this: that we obey His commands." This doesn't mean we love Him by obeying His commands. The Pharisees did that. Rather, our love for God leads us to trust Him, and when we trust, we naturally choose to obey.

We don't panic; we problem-solve. Like us, our children can either focus on the problem or be solution-oriented. Lilla tends to let the problem consume her. Panic has never solved anything. When an issue starts to block the possibility of a solution, we remind her of this phrase and encourage her to take deep breaths. Sometimes it's the small stuff, and sometimes it's bigger, but together, we work toward a solution.

You get what you get and are grateful for it. This one isn't new. It's a common phrase with a small twist. Originally, it would end with, "and you don't throw a fit." But it's always better to teach people how to win than to focus on how not to lose.

Will you forgive me? Saying "I'm sorry" is only part of the reconciliation process. We want our kids to be bold in taking the next step by asking for forgiveness, but we must first model this. Too many people resort to conflict games, passive-aggressive behavior, lashing out, or giving the silent treatment. Jesus didn't model this behavior, and it's not something Jennie and I want in our home. Our goal is to own our part and seek forgiveness quickly. The amazing thing is that Lilla might be the quickest to forgive in our home.

The list could go on, but you don't need me to spoon-feed it to you. All you need to do is identify the areas where your child needs to grow (look for patterns) and create an anchor statement that is simple, memorable, biblical, and age-appropriate. And just like that, you'll be teaching your child how to read the map as you journey against the flow of traffic toward a greater destination.

Reflection

1. What is the destination you are parenting toward?
a. Where do you want your kids, marriage, or relationships to be in five years?
b. Ten years?
c. Twenty years?

2. Is how you're living today going to take your family to where you want to go?
a. What needs to change?

3. What is your default vehicle to get to where you want to go?
a. Is it anger, disrespect, yelling, passivity, love, passive aggression, or simply dragging them along?

4. What mile markers have you recently passed in your parenting?
a. Did you celebrate them?
b. What are the mile markers ahead that you should be looking for?
c. How will you celebrate when you reach them?

5. How good are you at I Spy? Is your family invited to play with you? In other words, how clearly can you see God's fingerprints, and are you teaching your family to find them, too?
a. How can you make this a part of your daily journey with your family?

6. What are some things that you are regularly trying to teach your child (ex: sharing, kindness, helping, being generous)?

Challenge

Work together to create anchor statements for each of these topics. Keep them short, biblical, and practical so they resonate with your child's heart. Don't do this alone! Create a date night with your spouse, or invite a friend or mentor to do this with you.

It Takes a Village to Raise a Parent

Fun fact: our family is in the middle of the adoption process. The baby we're expecting is one we've been matched with, though we've never met the birth mom in person. Honestly, parts of it still don't feel real. If you're not familiar, private adoption is expensive—really expensive. I'm a pastor, and Jennie is a teacher, so we knew from the start we wouldn't be able to do this on our own.

As we prayed and asked Jesus what we were supposed to do, He reminded me of the story of Mary and Mary Magdalene heading to Jesus' tomb. At this point in Scripture, Jesus had been crucified, and the women were heading to His tomb to anoint His body with spices. As they walked, they asked each other, "Who will roll away the stone for us?" (Mark 16:3). Keep in mind, this wasn't just some pebble. It was a massive boulder blocking the entrance!

I imagine the two women just shrugged and kept walking toward their Lord, not knowing what to expect. But what a surprise they were in for! The stone was moved! God used this passage to completely wreck me. We had our own massive stone in the way. We had no idea how we would raise the money or what steps we should take. But it was clear God was asking us to move forward in faith. So, we shrugged, laughed nervously, and wondered how God would roll away the stone.

While researching ideas for adoption fundraising, one idea stood out: we'd buy a 1,000-piece puzzle and sell the pieces for $10 each. Every time someone donated, we'd write their family's name on the back of a piece. Once completed, the puzzle would be sealed in a double-sided frame and hung in the baby's room. On one side, we'd see the beautiful design, and on the other, we would see the names of everyone who helped bring our baby home.

Now, let me tell you—I am not a fan of puzzles. But this was a chance to love my family and raise the support we needed. I was all in. When the puzzle arrived, I opened the box and started working on it. That's when I discovered a problem. Half of the puzzle was the same shade of pink. I'm talking zero variation, just a sea of identical pink pieces. It was absolutely miserable. Every piece had to be checked one by one to find the right fit. Months later, I've spent an absurd amount of time on this puzzle...and I'm still not done. The only reason I've made it as far as I have is that I haven't done it alone. Early on, when I realized this was the puzzle from hell, I changed the location of my discipleship meetings. We started gathering at my house, and as we talked, we worked on the puzzle together. I even began inviting friends over specifically to hang out over the puzzle. On football Sundays, I'd set up my makeshift puzzle table—two plywood boards clamped over our daughter's art table—in front of the TV. A buddy and I would tackle the puzzle while keeping an eye on the game.

This is an essential component of parenting. Not the puzzle part. I've told Jennie I'm never touching another puzzle again. After this one is done, that part of my life is officially over. But parenting often feels isolating, as though the challenges are endless and impossible. We struggle because we believe we should have all the answers and fear that asking for help signals failure. These are lies we've internalized, drawn to us by the relentless tide of societal expectations. The truth is, we were never meant to navigate this journey alone.

Parents, I have some tough news. You'll never be able to put all the puzzle pieces together for your kid. You simply can't. There are too many pieces, and you're far too human. To become the parent you were created to be, you need other parents around you—people who will help you grow and thrive.

I need people in my corner who hold me accountable, celebrate my parenting wins, and gently address my parenting misses. Not with judgment or parent shaming—there's already enough of that in the world—but with genuine care and wisdom. I'm talking about trusted individuals who offer biblical counsel and help me figure out where the pieces truly belong.

Admittedly, this is a stumbling block for many of us. On what should we base our trust? How do we identify someone as trustworthy? The current pulls at everyone else just as it tugs at you and me. If you're looking for someone to trust, seek out those heading in the same direction, against the current. There are parents in your community who are deeply in love with Jesus and striving to grow as disciples. It's important to find them and build meaningful connections. A great starting place is your local church. If you don't have one, prioritize finding one. Yes, finding a church home can feel challenging, but difficulty doesn't diminish necessity. The foundation of a trusted individual must be built on the solid rock of a deep love for Jesus and His truth. Anything less will crumble as the waves of the current crash ashore. Trust isn't about shared talents, hobbies, or environments—though those can be pathways to connection—but about finding fellow disciples who are leading their families toward the same destination.

This isn't a call to blindly trust anyone. Always measure what you hear against Scripture. Even the most trusted individuals are just as prone to drift as the next person. They'll make mistakes, too, and when they do, it's your opportunity to show grace, be trustworthy, and support them as they grow as disciples.

Don't fall into the trap of trying to do everything on your own. When I do that, it's my pride convincing me that I shouldn't ask for help. But parenting the way we were designed requires humility and community. Only when we let go of our pride and embrace support can we parent as God intended.

About a decade ago, I bought my sister a birthday present—tickets to Frozen on Ice in Orlando. She loved Frozen, and it gave me a great excuse to make the three-hour drive to visit some friends in the area (don't worry, I made it this time). On the ride over, I had a specific prayer. I wanted to use the trip as an opportunity to share the Gospel with my sister. I hoped that she'd come to know who Jesus is and place her faith in Him during our time together.

As the trip unfolded, we had some amazing conversations about God, along with a few epic Disney jam sessions. We had an absolute blast. Frozen on Ice was incredible, she felt loved, and I cherished our time together. But there was one lingering frustration. By the end of it, my sister still wasn't ready to place her faith in Jesus. I left feeling encouraged by how our relationship had grown, but also a bit disheartened. I couldn't shake the feeling that I hadn't figured out how to fit that puzzle piece into the right spot.

Nearly seven years later, she sent me a text. Don't worry, we still talked in between—this was just a very specific message. It said something like, "Hey bro, I wanted to let you know that Joseph (her boyfriend, now husband) explained the Gospel to me in a way I'd never heard before. It just made so much sense. I wanted you to know that I've placed my faith in Jesus!" I read that text, and something in me broke. I was sitting in a staff meeting at church, crying as I praised God for His goodness. I must have looked like a madman, but I didn't care.

I could have responded differently. I could have been frustrated that she heard it from him and not me. I could have let my pride steal the sweet joy of that moment. I could have convinced myself that every puzzle piece was mine to place, but it's not. That's yet another lie that's easy to believe. The point of parenting, or even sharing the Gospel, isn't about putting every piece in its place ourselves. It's about working together to give each other a clearer picture of who God is. I had the privilege of baptizing my sister because some random, long-haired guy—now my brother—picked up a piece I couldn't and put it where it belonged.

You are not meant to do it alone.

In discipleship training that I've had the privilege of leading in my church, other states, and even other countries, we begin by asking a question: What is the first conflict we see in the Bible?

These environments typically include many church leaders, and some get excited at the opportunity to show off their Bible knowledge. I've heard answers like Cain going John Wick on Abel, or when Adam and Eve were banished from the garden, or even when they decided to trust a snake instead of God. Those are all great examples of conflict early in Scripture, but none of them are the first.

During the creation of everything, God followed a pattern. He would create something, and then He would say, "It is good." As He progressed through creating light, the seas, creatures, and man, He repeated this phrase each time. He did so until Genesis Chapter 2, where God looks at Adam and says, "*It is not good for man to be alone.*"

At this point, Adam was in perfect relationship with God. He had been given authority and responsibility in the garden, and he enjoyed the shade of the garden in the presence of his Lord. Yet, it was still not good. A deep, abiding relationship with Jesus is essential for good parenting, but it is not enough. Parenting in isolation isn't just hard—it's not good. We were designed for community.

I want to be clear. We are not talking about community for your child just yet. We'll get there, and honestly, that will likely be a response to the community you have for yourself. Right now, we're focusing on you having deep community

Parenting in isolation isn't just hard—it's not good.

with others who are in a similar life stage and are also in love with God. These are the people you'll lean on when times are tough, and you don't have the answers. They might not have the answers either. They may be just as confused as you are, both staring at the mess of puzzle pieces scattered on the ground. I've found that it's often less about having the answers and more about not going it alone.

The Box Top

When your child was born, they came with a faith puzzle that you are meant to help piece together. You'll play a key role in fitting the pieces into place and, eventually, teaching your child how to do it themselves. The only catch is that you received the puzzle without the most essential tool for solving it: the box top. The box top shows a picture of what the completed puzzle should look like. Since you've never navigated the parenting journey before, you have no idea what the finished picture is supposed to be. This leaves you uncertain about the final destination of the puzzle, making the task feel even more daunting. So, what can you do?

Borrow someone else's.

There are countless people in your life right now who have raised kids before and are a wealth of wisdom, offering insights into what worked and what didn't. This isn't to suggest that every child requires the same approach or that their faith puzzles will look identical. Once again, God's creativity calls for a personalized, anti-cookie-cutter approach. Your child is beautifully and wonderfully made, with a uniqueness all their own. Even identical twins are distinct individuals who need to be approached in ways that cater to their specific needs.

The colors of each puzzle may differ, and each child's passions and gifts will be unique, but the end goal should always point to the same thing. Regardless of the image on the puzzle box, the sole aim of every completed puzzle is clear: God's glory. Who in your life has been there before and has children who are now grown and deeply in love with God? Those are the people you should seek to partner with to help you understand how they nurtured a deep love for Jesus in their home. We don't need to be the blind leading the blind. We need to partner with those who have seen the box top and can guide us in understanding what the completed puzzle looks like. Don't believe me? Here's a challenge: Go to your local store, buy a 500-piece puzzle, and try to solve it… without looking at the box top. You'll quickly discover how difficult it is to identify the pieces you need without knowing and referencing the final image.

In 1 Kings, a man named Rehoboam ascends to the throne. Early in his reign, the people of Israel approach him with a straightforward request. They express that his father, Solomon, had been harsh with them, and the work and burdens placed on them had become unbearable. They asked King Rehoboam to lighten their load. Recognizing that the request was reasonable, the king told them to return in three days. During this time, Rehoboam made the wise decision that any leader should make—he sought counsel. First, he consulted the elders who had served under King Solomon. They advised him to ease the yoke on the people, promising that if he did, he would win their loyalty for life. What a promising start! This young king was on the right track, seeking wisdom from those who had worked alongside Solomon for years. They knew the big picture! But then Rehoboam consulted his younger friends. Not a good idea. They suggested that he should intensify the burdens on the people, even telling him to threaten them with even harsher conditions during his reign than they faced under Solomon.

Which group do you think King Rehoboam chose to listen to? His friends had no idea what they were talking about. They had never seen the box top and lacked a clear vision—especially in their youth—of what being a good, godly king meant. It wasn't wrong for Rehoboam to surround himself with peers, but it was unwise for him to heed their counsel while disregarding the wisdom of those who had a clearer perspective. Rehoboam followed his friends' advice and rejected the guidance of his father's elders, and as a result, his kingdom was divided.

Many of us hold a belief rooted in a lie. It goes something like this: "Don't tell me how to parent my child." This can also work in reverse, where people withhold counsel to avoid offending a parent or making them feel bad. I'm not suggesting you impose your parenting strategies on strangers in the grocery store. Don't be that person. Counsel is meant to take place within the context of a relationship. As Solomon says, "A wound from a friend can be trusted, but an enemy multiplies kisses" (Proverbs 27:6). Counsel might not always be what you want to hear, but a true friend will speak up to prevent you from stumbling.

Receiving this advice will require a Jesus-sized amount of humility. As parents, we must lay down our pride if we are to hear and benefit from this counsel.

If we aren't careful, we may misinterpret wise counsel as negative criticism. Statements like "You are failing," or "You're a terrible mom," or "As a dad, you're the reason your family doesn't look like the box top" are not how the Gospel works. Jesus is transformative; He is in the business of changing and redeeming. Did you fail? Maybe, but praise God that someone helped you turn things around. Did you have a bad parenting moment? It likely won't be your last, but how can you respond with humility and learn from it? Is your family drifting? The first step in correcting the course is recognizing the drift so you can chart a new direction. If you are my brother or sister in Christ, and we share a relationship, I expect you to speak into my parenting because there is too much at stake. I'm raising little kingdom warriors, and I want them to be ready to face the giants head-on, knowing they go with God.

Preparing your heart for counsel is important, but it's just the starting line, not the finish line. There's a difference between having the humility to receive counsel and the courage to seek it. There will be spiritual warriors who can help speak into your life. This isn't only true in parenting, but also in your marriage, your work, and your walk with Jesus. Many people have walked similar paths and tripped on the same stones. They want to help you navigate the journey and avoid the same pitfalls but don't want to impose them on you. If we are to use our communities for God's glory and the well-being of our families, we must invite counsel, not only for the big moments but in the routine. Sometimes, it could be as simple as asking someone you trust if there's anything they see in your parenting that you might be missing. If you give them permission (and some time to think it over), you're far more likely to receive counsel that could dramatically impact your family. Intentionally seeking advice and feedback from wise parents is like a burst of speed against the current, propelling you farther

> **There's a difference between having the humility to receive counsel and the courage to seek it.**

ahead than you could have gone on your own. It's one of the easiest ways to grow as a parent and one of the most underutilized opportunities. The value of being receptive to feedback is directly tied to your boldness in seeking it.

Often, it's our insecurity that prevents us from seeking counsel. We're so convinced that we're failing that we fear inviting someone to speak life might just confirm the lie that we believe. On the flip side, some believe they have it all figured out and don't need any help. Both attitudes are driven by pride, whether overtly or in the form of insecurity (pride turned inward). Pride is a dangerous current that will convince you you can breathe underwater until it's too late. The great irony is that our insecurity and pride often keep us from taking steps toward true security. We become paralyzed by fear. All that's required for the current to take you is for you to stop swimming. It will gladly handle the rest. Only when we humble ourselves and seek feedback from others do things begin to change. Here's a few:

1. We are practicing humility and battling our pride.
2. We create opportunities to be encouraged in the areas that we are crushing.
3. When growth opportunities are presented, we are given a target and can then identify when we are winning and where we need to make adjustments.
4. Insecurity and pride will fade into a humble confidence that can only come from being on a team that you trust.
5. Other parents will begin seeking counsel from you.
6. And still, you will continue to seek counsel from others.

Counsel is the reason an underqualified, stumbling dad like me can attempt to write a book on a topic as important as parenting. The majority of this book draws on the counsel and wisdom of the people in my community.

This isn't an invitation to unleash your parenting philosophy on an unsuspecting stranger in the grocery store. We've all been on the receiving end of unsolicited advice, and I think I can confidently speak for all parents when I say, "Not cool."

What I *am* saying is that we should be open to both giving and receiving counsel—when practiced in the right way. Discernment is key in this process. If the advice aligns with biblical principles, it can be trusted. But more often than not, what you'll hear is someone's personal take on what worked (or didn't work) for them—whether it's nap schedules, breastfeeding versus formula, discipline strategies, or a hundred other parenting dilemmas. While this kind of advice can be valuable, it's important to remember that not every suggestion will be the right fit for your family. Let God's guidance, honest conversations with your spouse, and wisdom from trusted friends help you discern what's best for your family. Take time to pray together—whether with your spouse or a trusted friend. No question or decision is too small or insignificant for Him. He is a trustworthy guide for you and your family. Some decisions will come easily, while others will require trial and error—and that's okay. You might try something, realize it doesn't work, and adjust course. The key is to stay open to wisdom while discerning which advice truly aligns with your family's unique journey. Listen, learn, and trust that God has equipped you to make the right choices.

As the saying goes, "Don't throw the baby out with the bathwater" (you know a phenomenal parent came up with that quote). Take what works, let go of the rest, and do so with gratitude. At the end of the day, you are the captain of your family's ship, and you know best what's needed to navigate your way upstream.

You desperately need a community in the same life stage to walk alongside and support you through the challenges of intentional parenting. Having a community within your life stage and seeking wisdom from those more experienced are not mutually exclusive; in fact, both are essential in the puzzle-making process.

You need help laying down the pieces regularly, but you also need to refer back to the box top to ensure you're moving in the right direction.

While Jennie was pregnant with our daughter, I made it my mission to seek out young adults who were deeply in love with Jesus. Whenever I found them,

I would meet with their parents, eager to glean any wisdom that could help me grow in my disciple-making journey as a parent.

I asked these parents what practices had helped them lead their families well and what they might do differently if they could go back. I had deeper relationships with some and felt comfortable asking if they saw areas in my life that needed change as I prepared to become a father. One of them even ended up discipling me, which proved to be an incredible step in the right direction.

As mentioned in previous chapters, it's hard to disciple our kids when we haven't been discipled ourselves. Being discipled by a spiritual parent could be the next step in your growth as both a disciple and a parent! Discipleship isn't just a word for a sign or bumper sticker. It's an action that requires commitment. Jesus personally discipled twelve men. He spent time with them, taught them, challenged them, rebuked them, ate with them, and asked them questions. The lead pastor at your church isn't discipling you simply because he preaches from a stage every Sunday. Your small group leader isn't automatically discipling you just because you meet weekly. Discipleship involves someone intentionally investing in your spiritual journey through regular, consistent meetings focused on your growth. This person will likely do with you the same things Jesus did with His twelve! If you've never experienced this, pray that God will lead you to someone with a relationship with Jesus that inspires you and ask them to help lead you closer to Him.

This won't prevent you from stumbling; and it certainly won't guarantee that everything turns out the way you hope. All you can do is your part. But I will say that it has been a tremendous help as Jennie and I have worked to lead our family well.

To Raise Tiny Disciples

My father-in-law, Eddie, is incredible. He has an unwavering love for Jesus, plays the drums passionately in worship at his church, and enjoys reading a good book. He also happens to be completely blind. When he first met my family at a restaurant, he told us he'd just bought a new mount for his rifle, called a scattershot. As we listened intently, trying to understand why this man owned a gun, he explained that the new mount worked great—all he had to do was point, and everyone would scatter. The room erupted in laughter, caught off guard by the man they'd just met making a clever joke about his blindness. All jokes aside, I've come to trust and admire this man deeply.

When Lilla was an infant, Eddie would hold her and walk around the house. I gave a man who couldn't see my newest love when she was most fragile, and I did so without fear or hesitation. I've known Eddie for eight years now, and in all that time, I've never seen him stumble. This man walks better than I do, and he's been walking with Jesus far longer than I have. All of this points to one thing: I want him to be someone who is helping carry our kids.

In the Bible, there's a scene where Jesus is teaching in a house so packed with people that they spill out into the street. Four men hear about Jesus and decide to carry their paralyzed friend to Him. It's the obvious choice. Jesus is performing miracles, and their friend needs one. So, they head to the house, but the place is overflowing when they arrive. They had come too far and carried their friend too long to give up now. They climbed onto the roof, dug a hole through the tiles, and lowered their friend right in front of Jesus. I can't help but wonder what the homeowner was thinking as his ceiling tiles were torn apart. Were they worried about the roof, or were they excited about what Jesus would do next? I like to think it was the latter. Regardless, the paralyzed man now lays at Jesus' feet, and Scripture says that Jesus saw THEIR faith and told him, "Your sins are forgiven" (Luke 5:17-39). Jesus didn't just see the man at His feet. He saw the faith of the men who carried him. They brought him to the point where he was forgiven and would soon pick up his mat and walk out of that place on legs that had once been paralyzed!

This is the beauty of community: it's not just for you. You're not the only one doing the work within a godly community. You need others to help carry the mat as you lead your child to the feet of Jesus. In doing so, we create a space where our children can seek counsel from other wise, Jesus-centered adults. Jennie and I can't be the only voices in our kids' lives. I want them to learn how to identify and seek guidance from other Jesus-centered adults who can offer wise counsel.

If you have family members who are deeply in love with Jesus, this is where they will truly shine. Empower them to build relationships with your kids and help shepherd your child's heart closer to Jesus. Carrying the mat is always easier when done together. This is especially true for grandparents. They can be a safe place for your child to turn to when seeking advice outside of their parents. If you have this, cherish it. It is both right and good for godly grandparents to speak into the lives of their grandchildren. Not everyone has this privilege. It may be because your parents don't have a relationship with Jesus and cannot offer that counsel, or perhaps they have passed away. Either way, it's vital to have people around you who can speak into your child's life. When a corner of the mat is missing a carrier, it's important to reach out and seek those who can help.

But this is only part of the picture! Our children also need other kids who are actively being discipled. Think about it. Where do our kids learn to share, love, and sacrifice? How do they learn to handle conflict or when to seek counsel? It's through the relationships around them. As I mentioned earlier, we are built for community. We are hardwired for it. You can help them build a healthy community—or not. Here's the problem: if you don't, they still will. But without your guidance, the community they build may not shepherd their hearts well. We just saw what happens when a community rallies around someone in need and brings them to the feet of Jesus. The man who was paralyzed is now doing air kicks through the marketplace. But what if the community hadn't carried him to Jesus? What then?

In John 5, we encounter another man at the Pool of Bethesda who cannot walk. There was a belief that when the water in the pool stirred, the first person to step in would be healed. The man waited by the pool, hoping for his turn every day. He had a problem and needed help, but without anyone to carry him, he tried to solve it on his own. But Jesus, in His pursuit of people, found this man anyway.

He approached him and asked if he wanted to be healed. The man explained that he desperately wanted healing, but every time he tried to get into the water, someone else beat him to it. When Jesus asked if he wanted to be healed, the man's answer was a request for Jesus to carry him into the water before anyone else. He hadn't been carried to Jesus by his community, and now he was seeking to be carried elsewhere to fix his problems. But Jesus didn't carry him into the pool because the pool wasn't what he truly needed. Instead, Jesus healed him on the spot and told him to pick up his mat and walk (John 5:1-15).

Jesus is in the saving business and doesn't need our help to save our children. However, He gives us the important role of carrying a corner of the mat and inviting others to do the same. Jesus often intercedes on our behalf despite our shortcomings, but that is no excuse to ignore the role He has called us to play.

When I was in college, I had no idea how to build a biblical community, nor did I truly understand what it should look like. I was "Jesus adjacent." I called myself a believer, but I had no real relationship with Him and didn't know where to start. I was caught in the dangerous position of believing in Jesus without placing my faith in Him. I sat at His feet, trying to devise my own plan for healing. I was lost. As confused as I was, I desperately craved community, and I found one in a fraternity. It was a group of fun guys who liked to hang out, and that's exactly what I thought I needed. They were incredibly kind to me, even during my most foolish moments. But despite their kindness, there was never a moment when that community pointed me to the God I so desperately needed. We were just a bunch of guys, sitting on the water's edge, waiting for the pool to stir. I thought I was where I needed to be, but I was simply paralyzed.

Many of our kids live "Jesus adjacent," searching for what it truly means to build community. But when conflict arises, they don't know how to handle it biblically, nor do the people around them. When stress hits, they don't know where to turn. Our kids will always seek to build community because that's how they're wired. The real question isn't whether they will pursue community. It's whether that community will help carry them closer to Jesus. Will their community help carry the mat, or just sit with them by the pool? If we don't show them the right way, they'll start piecing together their own version of community. It won't be pretty, and it won't be easy, but they will try to make a picture out of it. The picture I started to create in college looked nothing like the one Jesus had designed for me. My puzzle was one of self-glorification, driven by a passionate pursuit of whatever I desired. It became a self-portrait, one that had nothing to do with giving God the glory.

> **Will their community help carry the mat, or just sit with them by the pool?**

As our kids grow up in godly communities, they will face the same struggles as any other child. Sin nature is sin nature. I didn't have to teach my daughter how to lie. I get to teach her how to tell the truth. No child is exempt from this. However, it becomes much easier to teach our kids how to be young disciples when they're surrounded by other kids who are growing in the same direction. They will mess up, but as an intentional parent, you'll use those moments as opportunities to hold your corner and take another step closer to the Healer.

To be clear, a Godly community isn't about excluding kids who aren't being raised in Christian homes. Our daughter attends a public school and has many friends from different religious backgrounds and family situations. As believers, we are called to have deep relationships with those who don't know Jesus. However, the community we lean on should always glorify the Lord. In Acts 2:46, we see the disciples constantly gathering in each other's homes, breaking bread, and doing life together. I want our children to grow up in an environment where community is a natural part of life, not just a special occasion. They should expect people to come over because that's simply what we were created to do.

I don't know what happened to those paralyzed men after they met Jesus. I wish Scripture told us, but it doesn't. However, I do know a few things about people who are healed. I imagine they used their newly healed legs to celebrate the mercy God had shown them. I think (though I can't be certain) that after they were done leaping for joy, they would have walked up to others who couldn't walk, grabbed a corner of their mat, and started carrying them to the only one who could heal them. If you want to know the true victory, that's it. At some point, I have a holy expectation that our kids will step off their mat. As they do, they and everyone on each corner will rejoice in the wonder of what God has done. Then, our kids will find others still on their mats, grab a corner, and start to carry.

Reflection

1. Do you currently have a community in your life stage and what does it look like?
a. Are the people you are walking with able to carry a corner of the mat?
b. Have you invited them to?

2. What does the wise counsel in your life look like?
a. If your parents aren't an option, who in your life can step in?
b. When you receive wise counsel, are you humble enough to hear it?
c. Do you create opportunities for wise people to speak into your parenting? How can you?
d. Who do you need to invite feedback from right now?

3. Are there other trusted adults that your child/children can go to for help?
a. Do they have other like-minded kids that they can do life with?

4. If you are not being discipled, pray about who to ask and commit to a time to talk with them.

Challenge

Set aside intentional time, ideally with your spouse, friend, or mentor, to evaluate your involvement in a biblical community. Identify relationships where you'd like to invest more deeply and make a plan to strengthen those connections. For example, Jennie and I don't live near our families, but that doesn't lessen our need for a strong, biblical community. So, we created a weekly event called "Friday Family Dinner" with a few friends. Every Friday night, four families of varying life stages come together for dinner, laughter, and fellowship. Our kids enjoy spending time with their friends, and we are so grateful for the safe space to be with like-minded people.

Part 2:
What Now?

Fail Forward

One of my favorite football players to watch in his prime was Ezekiel Elliott. That guy was a one-man wrecking ball. While he wasn't always the quickest to dodge a linebacker or the fastest on the field, there was one thing he did better than anyone else. I'd watch him hit the line of scrimmage, get blasted by an incoming defender, and fall down for about eight yards. He didn't always break tackles or make a highlight-reel play, but he consistently gained more yards because he had an uncanny ability to fall in the right direction. He understood that falling was inevitable. So when you do it, you have to fall in the right direction—in football and in parenting. The trick isn't avoiding contact; it's about failing forward—consistently and often.

I make plenty of mistakes as a dad. Once, while we were at Ikea, I forgot diapers. I know. I know…rookie mistake. We were halfway through their in-store corn maze when our daughter did the unimaginable. It was horrific, and no diaper in the world stood a chance. Typically, exit signs mean you're close to an actual exit, but not at Ikea. Every exit ended up being the doorway to another department. It felt like an eternity before we found our way out. We laid down a towel and rushed to Walmart to buy diapers—and my wife a new shirt. Yeah…it was bad.

I make mistakes sometimes. Active parenting is filled with opportunities to learn and grow. It's not about doing it perfectly. It's about how God is glorified in our intentional responses to failure. In fact, it's through these simple imperfections that I declare my dependency on God. There's never been an expectation for us to be perfect, other than the ones we impose on ourselves. The law wasn't given so we could nail it. It was given to make our desperate need for grace abundantly clear. Your striving for perfection doesn't come from Jesus. Maybe it comes from a parent, a spouse, or the reflection staring back at you in the mirror—but not from Him. Yet, the lies are convincing, and the weight of perfection is an impossible standard looming over every parent. Failure rumbles like thunder, and shame echoes in its wake.

Adam and Eve lived in perfect harmony with God and each other. They had everything they could ever want or need, yet they chose to listen to a snake instead of God. The consequences of their choice were immediate: they became aware of their nakedness and ran to hide from their Creator. They had only ever known intimacy with God, but in their failure, they hid in shame.

When we fail as parents, shame sneaks in, convincing us to hide or defend ourselves. We can't show weakness or any sign that we don't know what we're doing. We feel like we need to be strong and act confidently, even though we're uncertain. As a pastor, I find this temptation especially intense. I'll sit in a small group, struggling with God because He's calling me to share something vulnerable with the group, but I'm the pastor. I can't admit that I was in an argument with Jennie the night before and dishonored God in how I spoke to her. I'm supposed to be the one with all the answers, the one who has it all figured out. But that's a lie. The enemy is so skilled at twisting the truth just enough to make us believe it. The most convincing lies are often just slightly twisted truths. It's true. I'm a pastor. It's true that I've made huge mistakes and, at times, treated my wife poorly. It's true that I didn't honor God in those moments. Therefore, I should hide. False! This temptation isn't limited to pastors or church leaders. It happens to all of us, and its results affect our work, our discipleship, and our parenting.

We often think that because we hold positions of authority or influence, we can't make mistakes—and if we do, we certainly can't admit it or let others know. The truth is we need to stop pretending we have it all together. We need to step out of the bushes and meet God—and each other—face to face. Shame tries to pull us into the bushes, but that's not where God is (unless it's on fire). He's in the garden, waiting for us to step toward Him, defying the steady pull of our shame. We need to be secure in God's grace for us to allow ourselves to fall in the right direction. Failing forward in our parenting means accepting our mistakes and bringing them into the light.

> **Shame tries to pull us into the bushes, but that's not where God is**

Our kids aren't immune to this either. We don't intentionally teach shame, but it finds its way into our kids just the same. I remember the first time we saw our daughter experience shame. She'd made a mistake, and her eyes dropped to the floor as she quietly cried. I kept gently asking her to look at me, but she could only manage brief glances before the weight of her shame pulled her gaze back to the ground. As parents, we don't need to teach shame, though we certainly have opportunities to reinforce it. But that's not how I want my daughter to live. Our kids are far too passionate and loving to be afraid to look the world in the eye. Failing forward can only happen when we're freed from shame. Your mistake is the fall. What you do with it determines the direction it takes you.

To combat shame, our family emphasizes clarity by distinguishing between mistakes and bad choices. A mistake (like spilling a cup of water) isn't based in sin. It's simply a symptom of being a kid in an adult world. We celebrate mistakes in our home, not because we want our kids to fail, but because we want them to take risks, try new things, and solve problems. Cake is the ultimate anti-shaming tool. When we celebrate our kids' mistakes—or more specifically, their courage in taking a risk—they learn without being owned by failure. Shame has no place at the party. A bad choice (like karate-chopping their brother because they both want the same toy) comes from sin nature or foolishness and requires correction. But in either case, our first response is always to battle shame. Let me be clear: Shame is from Satan, and it has no place in any of our homes (and neither does he). The way we lead and discipline our children must be free of shame. And honestly, this isn't always easy. How do you correct a child's behavior in a group setting? It's incredibly challenging, and I've seen three main options play out. You can choose to ignore the negative behavior, regardless of how it affects the group. You can put your child on blast in front of everyone. Or, you can gently pull them aside and address the situation privately. We need to be careful because a little bit of shame can fill a small heart.

This isn't about judgment. I've done all three, and I genuinely believe there are times to let it go (and possibly address it later), times to address it publicly (safety situations are a great example), and times to pull them aside for a one-on-one conversation. I tend to lean toward pulling them aside more than any other approach, but no matter the option, we must always measure our response against the potential for shame. I want each mistake or bad choice our children make to be an opportunity for them to experience deep love as they fall forward for a few yards. Maybe, just maybe, they'll even give Zeke a run for his money.

A Story of Shame

Jesus has given us a powerful tool to use as we disciple our children—and yet, we often hide it from them. Your testimony is one of the greatest weapons God has given you for His kingdom. He has transformed your story of shame into a testimony of grace, with His loving fingerprints all over it.

But this carries a crucial prerequisite: you must first be saved by Christ. Without faith in Jesus, you are still bound by death—and families weren't meant to be raised in tombs. Grace is waiting for you—a testimony written by His own hand, declaring undeserved mercy and redemption. And it's that same grace, overflowing from Him to you, that will pour into your children as you lavish them with the love and forgiveness you have freely received. Yet, testimonies aren't built in a day.

Have you heard about Lazarus (John 11:43-44)? The man was dead. #RIP. But then Jesus shows up, calls him out of the grave, and here's the crazy part—Lazarus actually comes out. New life had been given. But even though he had stepped into freedom, he was still wrapped in grave clothes. Those bindings had to come off.

Some of us have been ushered into new life while still carrying the baggage of our past. This is why, at first, your testimony doesn't feel worthy of fist bumps and air kicks. It feels messy. It feels heavy. It still smells like the tomb.

But here's what Lazarus didn't do: He didn't say, *"I don't deserve to be saved! I can't believe I ever went into the tomb!"* No. He stepped out. And then he went back to town, testifying about what Jesus had done. Part of me wonders if he carried those grave clothes with him—not to shame himself, but to show just how dead he was and how alive he is now.

This transformation isn't instant. Learning to accept grace takes practice. But hear me—you weren't saved for tombs, and your story isn't meant to stay wrapped in grave clothes. Your shame, guilt, anger, despair—all of it—can be transformed.

I've noticed that believers typically fall into one of two categories: either you're a recovered prodigal or a recovered Pharisee. The prodigal (Luke 15:11-32) is someone who ran after the world, made a mess of their life, and eventually realized their desperate need for Jesus. The Pharisee (Matthew 23) is someone who grew up following the rules, believing they were "good," only to later realize they never truly knew Jesus.

The prodigals often wish they hadn't made so many mistakes, while the Pharisees feel their testimony lacks value because they haven't had a dramatic event to make their story stand out. Here's the truth: your testimony isn't about the broken mess you once were. It's about the most beautiful rescue in history. Both stories are beautiful. One reveals how God redeems brokenness, the other how He breaks through self-sufficiency. Neither is better than the other—both are weapons for the Kingdom.

A messy testimony shows that no one is too far gone for grace. A quiet testimony shows that you don't have to wreck your life to realize your need for Jesus. And both can reach people that the other might not.

Your testimony, no matter what it looks like, has power. But when it comes to our kids, we often hide in the bushes, ashamed of what we've done. Yet, the very thing we want to conceal may be the exact thing God will use to bring them closer to Him.

My prodigal story has empowered me to reach other prodigals; to jump into the pit with them, and show them the way out. But a Pharisee might hear my story and struggle to see God's glory in it. My story isn't meant for some people. While some might find it difficult to relate, that doesn't mean I'm not called to share it. The recovered Pharisee may be better equipped to reach those who are blind to their desperate situation because, by all outward accounts, they are "good." This recovered Pharisee, whose story might seem boring to some, could be the one able to present the Gospel in a way that person is ready to receive. Your testimony is powerful—but when it comes to our kids, we often hide in the bushes, ashamed of what we've done.

Hear me. I understand that specific details need to be age-appropriate. My daughter doesn't yet know that, by God's grace, I am eleven years sober and a recovered alcoholic. Alcoholism is too complex for a 5-year-old to grasp. But one day, when she's old enough, we will talk about the idols I had in my life and how Jesus met me where I was, forgave me, and transformed my life. If I hide my past, I hide the miracle. I plan to share these parts of my story with my kids, not to focus on my mistakes, but to glorify God.

> **If I hide my past, I hide the miracle.**

I felt honored when I was first asked to share my testimony in our Young Adults Ministry small group. I was excited to share everything God had done in my heart. But that excitement didn't last long. A few days later, a coworker approached me and said he was finally planning to attend. I had been inviting this guy for months, and this was the Tuesday he chose!? Honestly, I was scared. I didn't want anyone at work knowing I was a recovered alcoholic. I didn't want to be judged, and I definitely didn't want that kind of news spreading around the office. I cared deeply about this guy and wanted him to encounter Jesus, but the risk felt too high.

So, I called Matt (like I've mentioned before, this guy changed my life) and told him I wasn't sure I could share my testimony anymore. When he asked why, I explained that I couldn't honor God while leaving out my alcoholism, but I was terrified of a coworker knowing my past. Matt could have let me off the hook or challenged me right then and there, but discipleship isn't about making decisions for someone. It's about empowering them to press into God and seek His guidance. So, instead of telling me what to do, Matt simply said, "Pray on it and let me know what God wants you to do."

Not long after that, I sat down with Jesus, bringing my fear to Him, and His response was clear. *"Who are you sharing this testimony for?"* Seriously, Jesus? Did You really have to convict me like that? It wasn't what I wanted to hear, but the path forward became obvious.

I called Matt and told him I believed God was calling me to share my testimony boldly for His glory, even with my coworker in the room. Here's the irony: the guy never even showed up. He flaked, but the lesson wasn't lost. My testimony isn't about who shows up or what they think of me. It's for the glory of God and the benefit of others.

Our children desperately need to see God's glory reflected in our lives.

My favorite story in the Bible is Acts 16. I shared it with my daughter on the drive to school this morning. There's so much more to the story than I can include here, but I'll give you the cliff notes version.

Paul and Silas were two men on fire for Jesus. At one point, Paul cast a demon out of a girl, which infuriated her owners (she was a slave—you'll have to read the full story to understand why). The situation escalated quickly, and before long, Paul and Silas found themselves in prison.

While they were locked up, something incredible happened. As the hours passed, Paul and Silas began praising God, their voices rising in song. The other prisoners listened intently. Suddenly, a powerful earthquake shook the entire prison. The doors of every cell swung open, and the chains fell off every prisoner.

The jailer, apparently jolted awake from a deep sleep, saw the open doors and panicked. Assuming the prisoners had escaped, he drew his sword, prepared to end his life, execution being the punishment for losing prisoners. But from within the cell, a voice called out. Paul said, *"Do not harm yourself! We are all here!"* (Acts 16:28).

I absolutely love that moment. They could have left. Freedom was right there, but not one of them moved. A greater plan was unfolding, and every prisoner in that jail was submitted to it. The jailer, amazed and confused, fell before Paul, asking what he needed to do to be saved. And Paul told him.

As incredible as this story is (and believe me, it's my favorite), that's not the main reason we're talking about it right now. The real takeaway comes in the next verse. Scripture tells us that the jailer and his entire household were baptized that very day.

How does that even happen? Here's what I think. The jailer went home and immediately shared what had happened. Do you think he skipped over the part where he had fallen asleep on the job? Do you think he worried about his reputation or what his family might think of him? Not a chance. His life had been radically transformed because he had experienced the grace and mercy of God.

And here's the kicker: it likely wasn't Paul who led the jailer's family to Christ. It was the jailer himself, through his testimony. As his family listened to his story, they likely saw God's power at work in his life, and they couldn't help but be drawn to start their own relationship with Jesus.

Your testimony holds incredible power for your family. It's not meant to be hidden or whispered in secret. Despite our mistakes, God's glory shines. It's in our brokenness that the world sees just how deeply we've been healed.

I get that sharing your story can be intimidating. For what it's worth, I just wrote about my alcoholism in a book with my name on the cover. If it were just about the disease, I'd be terrified. But my goal isn't to highlight the problem. It's to point to Jesus, the Great Physician. I want my kids and yours to know the Healer. Don't let your shame keep your story hidden. Let's show them how deeply we've been restored.

We've all stumbled. Maybe your shame feels like a 260-pound linebacker barreling toward you. But here's the truth: you can either be owned by your shame or surrender it to the only One whose shoulders are strong enough to bear it. Jesus knew exactly what He was paying for on the cross. Nothing about your past, your struggles, or your regrets surprises Him. He stands ready to take your shame and transform even your most painful, hidden, or embarrassing moments into a testimony of His grace and glory. What the enemy meant to keep you bound, Jesus is more than able to redeem. Share your testimony. Let your failures—your mistakes—help you pick up some yards for God's glory.

Conflict

If only our mistakes could stay locked in the past. Wouldn't it be great if Jesus gave us a powerful testimony and we never messed up again? I'd love to tell you I've never lost my cool in the middle of Target or neglected my family during too many football Sundays. But the truth is, I can't write a chapter about failing forward without being honest about my own shortcomings.

I'm convinced that as long as I'm alive, Jesus will always have something to refine in me to mold me into His image. My closeness with Him doesn't make me immune to mistakes, but it does shorten the time it takes for me to seek forgiveness. That's a key ingredient in failing forward, even in the stumble, you're gaining ground for Jesus.

We often don't know how to handle conflict, especially with the people closest to us, so we ignore it. We shove our frustration and hurt under the rug, even as it creates a mound we keep tripping over. Yet, we'd rather stumble over that mound than face the problem, acknowledge our pain, and take responsibility for our part. Instead, the tension spills out in passive-aggressive comments or disproportionate reactions to unrelated issues. Our inability to address conflict maturely and biblically is one of the biggest destroyers of relationships.

We often avoid conflict, caught in a rip tide mentality. When emotions are high, we hold back to avoid escalating tension. When emotions are calm, we avoid disrupting the peace. The result? Unresolved issues persist. We'd rather ignore the recurring offense to preserve a moment of tranquility. But Jesus didn't shy away from making waves. He consistently stood against cultural norms and artificial harmony to reveal truth. We can't use good times as an excuse to avoid addressing conflict and pain. We need to risk the good to pursue the better. If we're called to reflect His image in our homes, we can't hide from conflict.

To be clear, this is not a validation of your last blowup with your spouse over dishes or house cleanliness. Too often, Jesus' flipping tables in the temple has been weaponized as a justification for our flesh-driven reactions. Did Jesus flip tables? Yes, but He did it in response to idols being sold in God's temple. Most of the offenses we face at home are far from heretical. Being willing to make waves is not the same as destroying the people in your house.

I'm saying that we must be willing to address conflict directly. Hard conversations are, by nature, hard—it's in the name. Passive parenting will always favor walking on eggshells, while tyrannical parenting brings hurricanes with a "no survivors" mentality. However, a strong, Jesus-centered parent makes intentional waves that strategically push back the current and resolve recurring issues. We must be ready to face the hard conversations with our families.

At my church, we say, "We fight for relationship, not in relationship." When problems arise, our goal isn't to win the fight but to draw closer to each other through understanding, compassion, and empathy. How you handle conflict teaches your kids how they should handle theirs because, like it or not, they're watching.

If you and your spouse always fight behind closed doors, your children may learn conflict is something to avoid or hide. If you fight openly and ruthlessly, they may believe that fighting is about winning. Co-parenting adds even more complexity, as tensions often persist even when the other parent isn't present. Your kids pick up on more than you realize—not just what's said, but what's implied. But if you fight for your spouse, you model that conflict is about unity and reconciliation. It's about seeking to understand more than seeking to be understood.

This looks like drawing fewer conclusions and staying curious. The mark of biblically centered conflict is asking plenty of questions to genuinely understand the other person's perspective. This doesn't mean hearing them out and immediately conceding your position. It means letting love—not pride or any other driver of the flesh—be the foundation of the discussion.

As you fight for the ones you love, remember that you're only responsible for your part. The other person is responsible for theirs. Most of the time, my part begins with being willing to own my mistakes.

You will never succeed at this if your goal is to win. If we can't humble ourselves and openly admit when we've messed up (because, let's be honest, in most conflicts, we've done something), we're missing the point. We get caught up in this idea of being right. It's not even about being entirely right. We just need to feel more right, which makes them more wrong, and we win.

That's why we justify saying rude things because "they started it," or we raise our voices to the max because we believe our argument is more logical.

Lies. 1 John 3:16 says, "This is how we know what love is. Jesus Christ laid down His life for us. And we ought to lay down our lives for our brothers and sisters." Relationships were never about being more right; they are about choosing the other person over yourself. Too often, we position ourselves as adversaries in "better" positions, tearing each other down. But Scripture is clear: those who exalt themselves will be humbled (Matthew 23:12). There are tiny eyes watching, and they're learning how to handle conflict from us. Teach them well.

> **Relationships were never about being more right; they are about choosing the other person over yourself.**

One morning, Jennie and I found ourselves in a disagreement. We didn't use harsh language or attack each other sharply, but the tension in the room was palpable, and I felt myself becoming guarded. I'd tell you what the argument was about, but honestly, I don't even remember. What I do remember is that we were talking through something, and Jennie and I ended up on two completely different pages.

In that moment, I was all too ready to explain why I believed she was wrong. As a married couple, I'm not saying we always need to agree—in fact, constant agreement can be unhealthy—but I am saying that when we disagree, it's crucial that I choose to love Jennie and that we both remember we're on the same team. Unfortunately, that wasn't happening this time. I was laser-focused on the logic of my argument, but I was relationally and emotionally distant.

Then Jennie began to cry. It wasn't my best moment. As Jennie cried, our then, four-year-old daughter walked over to her and started gently rubbing her back. A little girl who still sleeps with a night light is already better at comforting than I am. Meanwhile, I continued presenting my logical, calculated points, explaining why I was correct.

Then my daughter got up from the couch, walked over to me, and whispered in my ear, "Dad, Mom is really upset. She's crying." I could have responded with pride and frustration, brushing her off and telling her to mind her own business. But there was one problem: she was right. In my desire to win, I had forgotten who I was supposed to be fighting for. In that moment, I had failed to be the spiritual leader God had called me to be. I realized I can be correct in logic and terribly wrong in my execution. I had to seek forgiveness, first from my wife and then from our daughter. I celebrated Lilla because it takes incredible courage for a child to gently tell the person "in charge" that he's missing it. It was humbling and encouraging to see that when I fell and fumbled the ball, she picked it up and continued in the right direction.

I'm not a big fan of silver linings. I think it's okay for hard things to just be hard. I don't feel the need, nor do I want, to tie a bow on something to make it seem nicer than it actually is. Still, there are major wins in this story that we shouldn't overlook.

One win is my daughter seeing me make a mistake. She needs to understand that being an adult doesn't make you infallible. I don't want her growing up thinking she has to be perfect. If that's her goal, shame will own her heart. Every mistake will feel insurmountable, and every victory will be hollow and fleeting.

If you asked my daughter if her dad makes bad choices and mistakes, she'd smile and say, "Yup." She knows this, and she needs to see what it's like for godly parents to struggle.

It's a win that she felt the freedom to gently correct her dad's shortcomings. It's a win that her heart is already so bent towards empathy and compassion. And it's a win that I could battle against my pride and show her what seeking forgiveness looks like. In many ways, these are the moments that define parenting and intentionally discipling our children. It's not a perfect science where you get it right every time. It's about taking a few yards at a time as we fail forward together.

Redefine the Win

Sometimes we become so afraid of failing that we avoid picking up the football altogether. It feels safer to stay on the bench than to risk getting knocked down. A few years ago, some buddies and I entered a charity fishing tournament. It was still pitch black when we got in our boat, and none of us knew what we were doing. There wasn't a real fisherman among us. As we set out on the water, I told the guys we might need to redefine what "winning" looks like. Yes, we were still aiming to catch a whale and see if Jonah was inside, but that wasn't the primary goal. If you're worried that this is about to turn into a justification for participation trophies, fear not. In a few paragraphs, you'll see that redefining the win means allowing our kids to lose. This isn't about avoiding the pain of defeat. Instead, it's about keeping the main thing, the main thing. We changed our definition of winning to having meaningful conversations about how we can grow deeper in our relationships with Jesus. We spent the day asking each other questions, catching up on our journeys, and not catching fish. I kid you not; I didn't catch a thing the entire day except a sunburn, and none of us reeled in a fish that stood a chance in the tournament. We felt incredible as we came ashore and drove back to the church for the winner's ceremony and meal. We'd had a total blast, each of us pressing into what Jesus had for us that day. Did we win the fishing tournament? No…no chance. Not even close. But it wasn't really about the fish anyway. Everything our kids do is an opportunity for them to learn about their Creator, to draw nearer to Him, and to understand who He says they are.

As parents, we desperately want our kids to succeed. I've even seen parents at their kids' games lose their cool over an umpire's call (you know who you are). We do this because we want justice and desire success for the ones we love. These aren't bad things. In many ways, they reflect God's heart for us. However, many of us have developed an unhealthy relationship with losing. We're terrified of it, and when it happens, it owns us. If we're not careful, it will own our kids, too. I believe one of the most important things we can disciple our children in is how to lose well. We want our kids to win so badly that we forget to teach them how to lose. Sometimes, we need to sit down, redefine the win, and seize the glorious opportunity to fall flat on our faces. The truth is, we usually don't know God's plan for any specific ballgame or whether He has a team preference. I guarantee He doesn't cheer exclusively for your child's team. He loves the kids in the other dugout just as much as He loves your kid. (Honestly, it'd be great if He became a Miami Dolphins fan, but at this point, that doesn't seem likely.) When discussing the Kingdom, your kid's game that feels so important right now, ultimately isn't as important as we think. However, the lessons learned within the game could have everything to do with your child becoming the disciple they were meant to be. What would be different if our hearts were more interested in what Jesus defined as a win?

> **We want our kids to win so badly that we forget to teach them how to lose.**

Here's what our kids need to know. If Jesus calls you to the plate and you step up in faith, if you hit a home run, you hit it for Jesus. And if you strike out, you strike out for Jesus. That's the win. It's not about the result, but about who you do it with. That's the real victory. It's not just about the outcome. It's about inviting Jesus to walk the journey with you. Win or lose, home run or strikeout, first place or last, "whether you eat or drink or whatever you do, do it all for the glory of God (1 Corinthians 10:31)."

In Acts, we meet a man named Stephen. Though his time in the spotlight is brief, he certainly shines while he's there. In Acts 7, Stephen is put on trial for boldly standing up for Jesus, and during this trial, he begins witnessing to everyone who will listen. It's an incredible example of boldness and strength. By all accounts, God had called him forward, and Stephen stepped up to the plate. The trial unfolded, and I picture a scene straight out of a gladiator movie, where the emperor raises his thumb sideways, and the crowd begins to chant, with the leader's thumb following their call. I can't say this is exactly how it went down, but it's not far off. The crowd wanted Stephen dead, and the leader (Saul... aka Paul) gave the signal. The mob picked up their stones and hurled them at Stephen until he was dead.

Not the most encouraging story, but wow. Stephen stepped up to the plate—and in the world's eyes, he struck out. He's dead. He didn't make it. But what if we saw this through God's eyes? There's a key part of the story I left out. As the stones flew toward Stephen's head, he completely ignored them. He saw something far more incredible and important. Heaven had opened up before him. He saw God, and next to God, he saw Jesus. Even as he was being murdered, he prayed for those who were killing him. Did he strike out? Everyone throwing fastballs for the Rockies (see what I did there?) would have said yes. But surviving that trial wasn't Stephen's win. His win was Jesus. Regardless of the outcome, he was willing to go wherever God called him. Philippians 3:8 says, "I consider everything a loss because of the surpassing worth of knowing Christ Jesus my Lord, for whose sake I have lost all things. I consider them garbage, that I may gain Christ." This passage makes it clear: a relationship with Jesus is the win. That's the target! That's the goal! Everything else, in comparison, is trash. Stephen understood this, but Saul did not. The best part is that Saul eventually met Jesus, and his heart and name were changed. He became Paul and later wrote this passage to the church in Philippi.

When our hearts are set on Jesus, the scoreboard becomes an opportunity to minister and love others well. I'm not saying you shouldn't strive to win. I'm a highly competitive guy, giving my all to everything I do. But I am saying that winning the game was never the most important victory set before us—and this truth holds for our kids, too. We need to give them opportunities to lose.

I play games with Lilla all the time. Sometimes she wins; sometimes she doesn't. We've paused many soccer games in the loft for a quick heart check. I'll ask her what's wrong, and she'll tell me she's mad because she's losing. I look her in the eyes and remind her I'm not up there for winning or losing. To be clear, there will be a winner and someone who doesn't win, but that's not my focus. I'm there to spend time with her. If it's just about winning, I'm not interested in playing. But if it's about spending time with this little girl who has my heart, then I don't care if I win or lose because it's not really about the game. At five, she's starting to understand that the game is secondary at best. Winning a game is never the most important thing. Failing is a great opportunity to teach our children how to lose with humility. When we do, we are discipling them to fail forward. We need to resist the world's definition of winning. The world was never meant to define the win anyway.

I recently heard a speaker share how her dad would ask her a question at dinner: 'Did you fail at anything this week?' If she said no, he'd be disappointed because he wanted his kids to take risks and feel free to fail. But if the answer was yes, he'd celebrate with her. This is a great example of how we can create spaces for our kids to know they're free to mess up. Here's the truth: if you're not perfect (and you're not), and they share your DNA (or they don't), chances are they'll mess up too. This is about helping our kids understand that falling doesn't mean they can't move forward. This is about showing our kids that their mistakes can't outrun God's grace.

Reflection

1. How do you view failure? Is it devastating or an opportunity?
a. How was failure viewed for you growing up?
b. What is your approach to failure teaching your kids?
c. What areas could you do a better job of failing forward?

2. How can you intentionally create opportunities for your child to learn how to lose well?
a. Where can you model this for them?

3. Is your testimony something that you hide, or is it a celebration of what God has done?
a. How can you take this celebration and invite your child into it? Vulnerability, authenticity, and honesty are essential here.

4. How can you leverage conflict as an opportunity to be humble and to model reconciliation?
a. Is there something that you need to apologize and ask forgiveness for?
b. When will you make time for this?
c. What is your biggest stumbling block in conflict?

5. Is it time to redefine the win?
a. Look at the different environments that your child is currently in and determine what kingdom-minded winning looks like.

Challenge

For Ages 2-8: Create opportunities for your child to practice losing. Don't be afraid to stick to the rules and win sometimes when you play a board game. It's not about crushing their hopes, but it's also okay to take the win. Before the game, define the win as quality time together. Afterward, debrief with them. How did they handle your victory in the game? How did they feel? Ask them how you could have shown them more love during the game.

For Ages 9 and Up: Share your testimony with your child. If you haven't done this in a while, practice on your spouse, mentor, or trusted friend first. When you share your story, do so with humility and honesty. While some details might need to be adjusted for their age, ensure that anything you leave out is for their benefit, not your own protection. Our kids need to see how God has worked in our lives.

Intentional Answers

Years ago, I was traveling with my church to Haiti for a leadership training. When we arrived, we were given a guide. I have been to many countries for a number of reasons and still, I've never been to one quite like Haiti. It is a combination of immense beauty and intense poverty. God's fingerprints are obvious, yet voodoo rules the land. During our stay, we never went anywhere outside of the compound without our guide. There were times where we would visit various villages and interact with the incredible people, but our guide was always nearby. His role was primarily to interpret, help us understand the culture, to answer any questions that we had, and to better equip us to be disciples in an environment that looked very different than our normal context. Several times, I wanted to understand something about Haitian culture, and I used my guide as a resource to better interpret what was happening before my eyes. Our guide was relationally driven and easily approached, so I went to him with every question I had with a deep desire to learn. Everything I saw was different and I wanted to understand…why…

What is a three-year-old's favorite word? *Why.* To them, everything is fresh and new and exciting. Every piece of the world we take for granted, they experience with the kind of awe that always gives my heart pause. Every time my daughter sees an airplane and waves, I stop and admire the wonder that she gets to live in every day. God's fingerprints are so visible to our children because the things that are normal to us are still new to them. Everything is exciting and must have some sort of significant relevance in the order of all existence, which brings us back to the word that parents dread…Why?

For many of us, this is the most frustrating word that our kids learn to say. If they are toddlers, they use this word every second to gain a deeper understanding of the things we view as trivial. Our teenagers use it so strategically that we can't help but feel as though they are insurgents challenging us to a duel in an effort to usurp our authority. As parents we hear this word more than any other and it can really get under our skin. I mean, who hasn't responded with "because I said so" just like your parents did? It's a quick and easy way to write off their questions to bring ourselves back a semblance of peace. We become even more authoritarian in our use of this phrase if we feel disrespected. We shout it as a declaration that my authority goes, no matter what. Don't question it. Our kids ask us "why" for a number of reasons, but the biggest is because they need a trusted guide to help them through this world.

If our guide hadn't been receptive to my questions while we were in Haiti, my entire experience would have been vastly different. I would have stumbled around in places without a solid cultural understanding, and eventually, I would have stopped asking questions altogether. I may have asked a friend or jumped on my phone to find the answers I desperately wanted. I don't want to be an inconvenience, and I would rather stumble my way through than ask questions to a person who will make me feel like a nuisance.

Even early on, we communicate with our kids whether or not we are a safe place for them to come with their questions. It may start with questions like, "why does the grass get tall?" But it doesn't end there. These questions quickly shift to "Why does God let people get sick?" and "How do I know God is real?" We need to be faithful in the rapid fire, silly questions to show our children that we are guides they can come to with their bigger ones. Every time you answer a question, you are telling your child that they can or can't approach you with more. If we shut down their small questions, they won't bring us their big ones.

> **If we shut down their small questions, they won't bring us their big ones.**

But Josh, I don't know all the answers! Amen. Neither do I! That is the challenge with the awe that our kiddos live within. They ask questions that we never thought of asking! Which leads us to the words that every parent, disciple-maker, and person of authority are terrified of having to say… "I don't know." We would hate to be the guide that doesn't have the full picture of the path and yet, that is so often what we are. We become so fearful of not having the answers that we begin to communicate to our kids that we are not a safe place for their questions while simultaneously making them feel foolish for asking a question that is equally mysterious to us. "I don't know," is a completely appropriate response especially if you do, in fact, not know. However, our role as disciple-makers doesn't allow us to leave it there. "I don't know," is the starting point into a wonderful adventure of new discovery for both of you.

A couple of years ago, a dad came up to me on a Sunday after I had given the message at our church. He had questions about God but more specifically, he was struggling in his parenting. I offered to get lunch with him to better understand what was happening. As we talked over lunch about his life and family situation, he began to spill the beans. His daughter had been asking him about getting baptized and he was hesitant. As I asked about his reservations, he stated that she could not articulate the reason that baptism was important for her faith journey, and because of that, he believed she was not ready. I didn't disagree, but I had two more questions for him. I asked if he knew the purpose of baptism and how he expected his daughter to learn the correct answer. He shrugged and said that he didn't know the point of it all and that he was hoping she would tell him. We get it so backward sometimes. We so badly don't want to have the wrong answer that we opt to give no answer and our kids pay for it. We pay for it! This was an opportunity for him to intentionally disciple his daughter. They could have pressed in together and both learned and grown together as they each took steps to press into Jesus. But it is easier to hide in the "I don't know" than to face it head on.

This means that we need to battle the spiritual equivalent of "because I said so," which is (as the Sunday school song would have us sing) "because the Bible tells me so." I don't say this to diminish the authority of God's word. The Bible is an inerrant resource for us as we delve into a deeper understanding of God's character and the purpose for our lives. However, this phrase is often a spiritual copout when we don't know the answer or don't have the patience to walk through it. Also, this response isn't actually an accurate answer. It may be how you know something, but it is not why it is important. Think about it. Your child starts dating someone who is not a believer. As an intentional parent, you have a conversation with him and share that you think dating her is a bad idea because the two of you are not equally yoked (like oxen, not an egg). They respond, "Why is it such a big deal?" What is your response? Is it that when oxen are not equally yoked, if they are of different strength and different maturity, one of the oxen will drag the other along until the weaker one dies? Is it that Scripture gives us wisdom on this and points to this being a hindrance to the journey of both people? This could be your response, but many parents are just as likely to say "because I (or the Bible) said so." This would be the equivalent of asking your tour guide why the group has stopped at a particular destination and having them respond, "Because it is on the itinerary." We can do better.

One of the greatest parts of discipleship is that as I disciple, I am constantly growing and learning, too. It is not uncommon for me to be in a discipleship meeting, becoming convicted on the same issue my brother in Christ is also struggling through. In fact, I contend that until you intentionally disciple someone else, the level of spiritual maturity you can reach and your intimacy with Jesus that you can experience are both capped. Don't put a ceiling on your spiritual maturity. Discipleship isn't just about them growing but it is going to grow and stretch you too. This is why we need to say "I don't know" more and why we cannot leave it there. The correct response goes something like this, "I don't know, but let's find out together."

Teenagers often leverage their "whys" a little differently. It can look more like you asking them to empty the dishwasher and they respond with that dreaded, rhetorical declaration… Why? We puff up our chest and react in anger because we feel significantly disrespected. Admittedly, sometimes you have been. Tone matters, but I would say that the question in itself is not rude. It's actually a wise question that you ask yourself every day.

The "why" is the thing that gives the "what" value. In other words, you can do the right thing with the wrong heart, and it is worthless. We do this all the time with God. We easily take the creator of the universe and turn Him into checkbox Jesus. If I do these things, I've done enough for Him. Lies. In Revelation 2, God is speaking to the church of Ephesus, and He lists out all the deeds and Godly accomplishments of the church. It sounds like a wonderful review until He says, "Yet I hold this against you; You have forsaken the love you had at first. Consider how far you have fallen! Repent and do the things you did at first. If you do not repent, I will come to you and remove your lampstand from its place," (Rev 2:4-5). Quick recap: God is saying, "You've missed it! You are doing all these awesome things, but you've forgotten your first love. You've forgotten WHY you do it! You cannot be my church without me. Get back to the love you had at first or I'm going to remove your platform." God doesn't look at your spiritual resume, He looks at your heart. The "why" matters.

Jennie and I (like most parents) are big fans of our daughter cleaning her room. There have been ages where she has needed significant help, but she's always participated. She has put up resistance at times, but it usually boils down to her heart. It would be easier to expect our daughter to clean the room because "I said so" and if she didn't, there will be significant consequences, but we have chosen a different path. Reminder, I am not against consequences. Consequences are a biblical concept that our children need to understand. However, before we declare their sentencing, we are meant to shepherd. Although I leverage consequences (and grace) strategically, I fight for them not to become the "why." In other words, I don't want my daughter to clean her room or to do the dishes because she is afraid of what will happen if she doesn't. And I don't want her to shirk her responsibilities because she expects grace (which in this instance, would truly be passivity). Your parenting always teaches your kids theology (good or bad). You're an earthy picture of our Father in heaven. If we aren't careful, our actions can communicate, "Do the right thing or get in trouble." No wonder kids grow up with a warped view that God eagerly waits to hit them with lightning bolts when they mess up. The "why" in our house is different. We want our daughter to clean her room, be respectful, and obey because she loves us. Obedience, trust, respect, responsibility, and kindness are simply a loving, relational response. Because of this, when facing opposition from our kids, we should prioritize and focus on the relational consequences before the physical ones. I want our children to tell the truth not because they are afraid of losing tv time, but because they don't want to break my heart. Love should be the "why" that drives every what (1 Corinthians 13).

We are each hardwired to look at the physical cost first, but that is not biblically what we were designed to do. We even do this with heaven and hell. When you think of hell, you likely imagine a fiery, not so great place that you don't want to visit. But the fire isn't the most important piece! It's about relationship with Jesus. You were made to be a son or daughter of the King. We were meant to be adopted into His family and when we deny our birthright, we become relationally separated from Him for all eternity. What if Heaven was a place of difficulty? I think Scripture is clear that it won't be, but pretend with me for a moment. Would you still choose heaven? My hope is that our answers wouldn't change because the physical stuff pales in comparison to the relationship that we gain. Even if heaven were painful, relationship with God would be well worth it! How can I say that? Let me tell you about a guy named Moses.

God had sent Moses to free a stiff-necked people who constantly messed up. God used him to provide signs, cut a sea in half with his sweet staff skills, and bring God's law to His chosen people. God was Moses' guide through this entire process as the Israelites constantly complained and asked "why" as they moved their way toward the land that God had promised. At one point, God stated to Moses that the Israelites were to enter the Promised Land alone and that God would drive away their enemies. They were to go alone because they were a stubborn people and God was displeased with them. What would you do? I feel like most of us would sprint toward the land of milk and honey, leaving God in the dust. It's a pretty sweet deal! God handles the bad guys and we set up shop in the land of promise to forge our own way.

We do this all the time. We choose NFL Sunday Tickets, paychecks, and the latest fashion trends over our time with God. Moses had this chance to seize God's incredible promise minus one thing: His presence. And Moses' response was simple. "I will not go." I will not go to a plentiful land without the one who designed it. I will not choose the physical over the relational. Relationship was always meant to be the most important thing. The physical cost for Moses making this decision was extreme! The Israelites were about to wander the wilderness for forty years. They were going to be dissatisfied, and revolts against Moses were going to be a regular occurrence. And after all that, Moses was going to get to the edge of the promise without being allowed to step foot in it. Yet, knowing all that, I'm confident Moses would have kept his answer. There was a promised land, but the real promise is a relationship with God. He couldn't have the land because He preferred the better option.

Just thirty minutes ago, I found out that my daughter told me a lie. It wasn't a big one, but it still happened. It's amazing how God is using this writing to remind my own heart. I got on her level and asked why she had been dishonest. She sniffled a little, apologized, and said that she really wanted to do what I had asked her not to do. She asked if she was getting consequences and I smiled. "It's not about consequences, honey. It's that my heart wants to trust you and when you lie, it hurts." I think that was harder on her than any consequence, so I looked her in the eyes as shame tried to sneak in and said in a low voice, "I love you. You can't "bad-choice" your way out of my love. I want you to make good choices because it tells me I can trust you, but even when you mess up, you have my heart." Yes, there was still a consequence for her choice. As I intentionally prayed through the situation, I believed there needed to be a consequence, but that was not the point of the conversation. It's little opportunities like this in which discipleship really happens. It's not all glorious, life-altering events, but a step-by-step journey as you follow your Guide against the current of this world.

Celebrate and Repeat

One summer during our middle school years, my twin brother and I went to a Boy Scout summer camp. It was a ton of fun! We had the chance to face all kinds of challenges and even some fears. Every trooper (is that what we were called?) was given a list of tasks at the beginning of camp and anyone who achieved them all would receive an award. I've never been in the business of doing things alone, so I rallied the troops! I got our group together and presented my plan. I had mapped out the camp and was strategic in ensuring that we achieved the tasks as efficiently as possible. I wanted them to know that I had a good idea and that we could finish all the tasks in just a few hours. This was my invitation. Join me as we help each other achieve this award. Honestly, I don't remember the name of the award, but I will never forget the story. You'll see why.

Nearly everyone in my troop was bought in on the plan, and we set out to knock it out that Wednesday. We went from place to place, station to station, ensuring everyone successfully marked off each challenge. Sure enough, within a few hours, we had all completed everything required and had qualified for the award.

On the last night, we waited patiently for the award ceremony. I still remember where I was sitting in that room. We were so excited and honestly, I was really proud. When it was time for awards, the camp director started calling names of the people who were receiving their pin. There were a couple of people from most troops, but our troop was different. When they got to us, they set up camp. One by one they invited each member to the stage to receive their award. I watched as every member of our troop was called forward. Every single one…Except me. They got to the end of all the awards and my name had not been called. I sat there silently not wanting to make a scene, but in my heart, I was hurting. As the camp director moved on to the next section of the night, I felt forgotten, left behind, abandoned. Then my dad stood up. It wasn't his turn to talk, in fact, I don't think the camp directors even knew who he was, but to him, that didn't matter. Where many dads may have chosen to remain quiet and address it later, my dad wasn't going to miss his chance. He stood in front of a group of strangers and told them how proud he was of his son. He smiled as he said how ironic it was that I was the name that was missed because I was the one who had made sure that our entire group achieved this award. He called me forward and publicly told that group that he was proud of me and then, he gave me my award. I don't know how my paper was the one that was lost, but I am grateful for the memory of my dad being proud of his son. Public attention isn't a one-size-fits-all solution. What makes one child feel cherished might make another uncomfortable. God doesn't work with cookie cutters. He crafts each of us uniquely. Every child needs celebration, but the way they receive it will differ. Take the time to learn how your child best experiences encouragement, and you'll discover the most meaningful way to celebrate their victories.

That experience shifted something in me. I started to believe in that moment that I was meant to be a leader. The truth is, it had nothing to do with an award. I doubt I would have remembered the ceremony at all had my name been on the list like everyone else's. In the grand scheme of my life, that award doesn't matter at all. It's not about the award. The part that changed me was getting to see how proud my dad was of me and how he wanted everyone to know it.

There is a discipleship principle here that we cannot afford to miss. What is celebrated gets repeated. When we celebrate someone, we are giving them the courage that they need to do it again. We are declaring to them and anyone around that they are winning, that we are proud, that we delight in them. I have a buddy who says that one of his biggest targets in parenting is that his child always knows that he is loved and that he makes his dad proud. As we intentionally disciple our kids, they are going to make some big mistakes. I'm talking, absolutely massive. But they are also going to do things that you want repeated (even in the midst of those mistakes). It is on us to find chances to celebrate the things that we hope are repeated.

What is celebrated gets repeated.

I was discipling a young man that shared with me that he had previously enjoyed stealing from our local grocery store. He even mentioned that he would often have the money but would choose not to pay. As he shared this, I knew it was time to celebrate.

What!?! Celebrate? What on earth could be celebrated? This dude was the Robin Hood of candy bars minus the part where he gave back to anyone. He was risking his future and his reputation over chocolate! How could celebration be the initial response?

You heard me. It was time to celebrate.

In that moment, this young man decided to take his sin out of darkness and to expose it in the light. He chose to risk with me, knowing that I could do any number of things with that information that could hurt him tremendously. He was saying, "Josh, I trust you with this." He was vulnerable, honest, and took a risk. He was taking a massive step against the current and toward Jesus. I wasn't going to miss a chance to celebrate the crap out of this dude.

After I celebrated the things that I wanted repeated, I challenged him. We talked about what biblical reconciliation looked like and I asked him to go home and pray about what he felt like God was calling him to do. He did. The next time we met, he had a plan. He was going to go into that store, find a manager, and confess what he had done. YES! This is incredible. I told him how brave he was being and prepared his heart because we did not know how this manager was going to handle his confession. He could instantly forgive, he could ban him, or he could even involve the police (after all, this was a confession of guilt).

Then, we jumped in my car and drove to the store. I watched as this young man walked up to the manager and confessed his sin. I also watched as the manager charged him $50 for the past things that were stolen. I loved it. He went up to the man and asked how he could make it right, and then he did what was asked of him. When this young man got back into my car, I was bursting with energy! As excited as I was about the steps that he had chosen to take to reconcile, we weren't done. He also needed to tell his parents so that they could intentionally walk beside him and hold him accountable. He told me that he would talk to them that week and would let me know how it went. I called his dad that day. No, I didn't share what happened. That wasn't my story to tell. I did, however, challenge his dad. I told him that his son was going to share something difficult with him, but that there was huge victory in it. I reminded him that he should be very proud of his son and even though trust might be impacted and there may be consequences, I wanted him to remember to celebrate the win. Kingdom ground was being taken in his son's heart! This was a chance for this father to tell his son that he can't fail his way out of his dad's love. This was a chance to say that he was there for his son, even when his son really botched it. Will there be consequences? Probably. But there will never be an absence of love.

There seems to be a brokenness in us that leads us to focus on the bad. It's so much easier to remember the negative comment that you heard years ago, than the compliment you were told yesterday. Something about us wants to dwell on the negative, but intentional parenting requires celebration.

In the parable of the lost sheep, Jesus shares about a shepherd who had one hundred sheep, but one had gone missing. This shepherd leaves the ninety-nine to go after the one and when He found it, he didn't shout at it in anger. He didn't beat that lost sheep or drag it back to the other sheep. He didn't punish it publicly so the other sheep knew to avoid wilderness wandering and he didn't tie the sheep up so it could never leave again. The good shepherd found the sheep, put it over His shoulders and carried it home and when He got home, He called together His friends and family and they celebrated. He wasn't rejoicing that the sheep had gone missing. He was celebrating that the sheep had returned!

Drifting and wandering are a part of living in a fallen world. I'm not justifying it. Drifting and wandering are not positive things worthy of your pursuit. However, as parents we need to guard our hearts and be prepared for it. Your child is going to wander. Their legs are still new, and they want to see where those bad boys can take them. When we identify their wandering and prepare to bring them home, don't forget to celebrate the victories. Celebration tells them what can be repeated and will encourage them to come home sooner.

React or Respond

Lifeguards have a very specific protocol during an active drowning. They don't swim straight toward the person but will approach (whenever possible) from behind. They'll clearly communicate everything they are about to do and always ensure they have their own flotation device. As they approach the victim, they need to be incredibly cautious for a very important reason; People who are drowning panic and react out of desperation. In their panic, they're likely to grab at anything and everything, including the person trying to save their lives, leaving both people at risk of drowning. The lifeguard is aware of the risk, which is precisely why they are taking the appropriate measures in advance. It's the best chance of survival for everyone involved.

My challenge as a parent is shepherding my child's heart while guarding my own. Sometimes, I can become frustrated by feeling wronged or disrespected, and I am prone to stumble in my anger. It's funny. We teach our daughter to step back, pray, and take deep breaths when she is overwhelmed or angry. Solid advice that I rarely take. As parents, we have the choice to react or respond when our child decides to push us to our limit. Reacting is a near thoughtless action that lacks intentionality and is often driven by emotions (primarily anger and fear). It occurs when my feelings take over and I speak or act without first following protocol. We can continue to react, or we can have a plan.

What if, instead of reacting, you chose to respond? What if you had a meticulous plan to ensure that you were guarding your heart and shepherding your children as effectively as possible? We need to be the lifeguard, not another drowning victim. We need to have a strategy to approach and direct our kids without allowing them to pull us under. Every good lifeguard has a way to stay afloat. Unfortunately, in conflict, we don't have any physical means to place our weight on as the waves of our child's emotions threaten to pull us below. We have something better. As disciples of Jesus, we have the Holy Spirit living inside of us. This empowers us to lean on God regardless of the wind and waves trying to pull us down.

There is a story in Mark 4 where the disciples of Jesus are on a boat during a horrible storm. As things became worse, the disciples believed that the ship was surely about to go under. Nothing that they did could conquer what the storm had to offer. In desperation, his motley crew went to the stern where Jesus was sleeping on a cushion. I absolutely love that part. Mark isn't known for being the most detail-oriented Gospel writer and yet, he wanted us to know that Jesus wasn't just sleeping in the storm; He was asleep on a pillow. He was comfortable. While everyone else was in a panic, He was at peace. The crew quickly woke Jesus and informed Him that this was it. We are going under. We had a good run. Jesus woke and told the storm to calm it down. We could stop there, thinking that the disciples nailed it. They were in trouble, and they ran to Jesus. Seems legit. But it continues. Jesus turns to them and asks, "Why are you so afraid? Do you still have no faith?" You saw the storm and you reacted! You reacted out of fear and doubt. In other words,

You forgot that Jesus is in the boat!

This is our problem as our child has a meltdown and their world ending quickly becomes our own emergency. The storm rages and in their panic, they begin to pull you beneath the surface. But what if we didn't let them? What if the disciples responded and remembered who was in the boat? I'll bet they would have acted a little differently. I expect that they would have been more likely to go to the stern, pull up a cushion and take the chance to get some rest next to the guy who could talk to storms.

I'm not saying we ignore our kids as they go off the deep end—please don't hear that. I'm just wondering why I am so prone to allowing anyone to steal my peace and joy. I don't think our kids were ever meant to have that kind of power, and they certainly are not mature enough to be trustworthy with it.

Jesus is the answer. He is in the boat and undeterred by the storm. He is the one who can stop it, but He is also the one who can sleep through it. I am a much better parent when I remember this and press into relationship with Him. As I do, I tune into what the Holy Spirit is speaking to my heart. In other words, "Holy Spirit activate!" If God is the one keeping your head above water, no storm can drag you down. This is true in your marriage, with your friends, with your enemies, and with your kids. We need to respond and not react. We need to remember who is with us in the boat and when we do, no one will have the authority or power to steal our peace.

Practice "No," Practice "Yes"

I can't say that this strategy started with the best heart. In fact, I think it initially originated out of my own selfishness and pride. Every parent has been there. You walk over to the pantry (or as my daughter has named it…the food place) and grab the twinkie (sub in your favorite treat here) you have been craving all day. This is your moment. You unbox this magnificent treat, sit down on the couch and take your first bite of high calorie goodness AND… in charge of your 5-year-old! You quickly hide the remains of your half-eaten, pre-dinner dessert to ensure this little predator doesn't know what you are up to. Too late. She's on to you. She can smell your fear! Do you continue hiding it? If not, you'll have to give her one too..

Obviously, this is hyperbolic, but the situation is not that uncommon. The first time this happened to me, I shouted something like, "I will not snack in fear" and proceeded to eat my treat without regard to the risk of our 2-year-old entering full-on Godzilla mode. And this might sound unkind, and truthfully (as previously admitted), I can't say that this started with the best heart posture. But as I worked through this with Jesus and as I have seen the fruit in our daughter, this is one of the best things that we have done as parents

I'm not talking about snacking strategies.

I'm talking about leveraging opportunities for our kids to hear and understand the word "no."

And hear me, this is a huge risk. You are risking your night, your peace, your quiet, your rest, your reputation as you deal with a meltdown in the craft section of Target, and your sanity! But we can either focus on the short view of what we risk now (listed above) or the long view of what we risk in the future (an adult that is entitled, prideful, and unwilling to be led). I have found that parents are going to pay the cost (and children too). It's up to you if you want to pay now or later.

It's up to you if you want to pay now or later.

If you're co-parenting, teaching your child to say "no" can feel especially challenging. Your time with them is limited, and you have little control over what happens when they're with their other parent. It's easy to slip into the role of the "yes parent," sometimes without even realizing it. Deep down, you may feel like you're in competition for your child's affection. You might even catch yourself thinking—or saying out loud—*I just want to win.*

That feeling is real, and the pull toward it is strong. But parenting isn't about securing our own comfort or validation. It's about raising up tiny disciples. That's why open, intentional communication with your co-parent is crucial. You may not always like them, but they are still your teammate. Instead of competing, start collaborating (as best you can). Your child doesn't need two opposing forces fighting for their love—they need two steady guides leading them well.

We have a rule in our home that Lilla is always allowed to ask the question "Why?" She must obey first, but she has permission to ask the question. Sometimes, she will ask why I said "no", and I will have a very specific reason, but other times I simply tell her that I am saying "no" so she can practice hearing it. The crazy part is that we have gotten to the point where I will say "no", and she will respond with "okey-dokey." It's literally one of my favorite things. Our daughter isn't perfect. This response occurs around 70% of the time. She still has room to grow (as do I). The point is that she is learning and maturing.

Why should our children practice hearing "no"? I'm glad you asked

Scripture is very clear when it comes to our role with people who have authority over us. We are called to submit to them, provided it doesn't go against what God says (Heb 13:17, Rom 13:1, 1 Pet 2:13). Our children need to know how to submit to the authorities that God places on their lives and that is first learned through the parent/child relationship. I am not saying that they will never lead. Our daughter has a ton of leadership potential and I believe she will be an incredible leader someday. But the mark of a good leader is that they are a good follower (Joshua and Esther are great examples of this). Regardless of the leadership roles that our children take on, they will still need to be willing to submit to God.

But if you practice no, it is essential that you practice yes.

"Wait, what?" Hear me out.

Balance with a "yes tilt" is required.

Not only are we risking peace when we say "no" but we also have to be incredibly intentional about saying "yes" (especially in reference to things that will grow our relationship). This part is absolutely essential. When I am tired from work and want to rest and she asks me to play soccer with her in the loft (we haven't broken anything…yet), I need to say "Yes," more than I say "No," because that is an activity that brings us closer together. I want her to know I am not someone who just says "no." I am someone who loves her and she can trust that my answer has her heart in mind. I want my daughter to practice hearing "no" and still hear "yes" more.

Balance with a "yes tilt" is required.

I have painted more than one Miami Dolphins-themed unicorn because of this tilt. I want to be clear. I didn't want to do it. I dislike art (mostly because I'm terrible at it). But I love my daughter. It is that love that needs to drive us. Being a parent is exhausting. Being intentional while parenting is even more so. But practicing "yes" is vital in building effective relationships with our kids.

The other day, my daughter was playing outside with a bucket of water and the mermaid toy she was given for her birthday. As I watched her, I remembered one of my favorite memories was playing football in our front yard with my brothers in the rain. Football wasn't the play here, but I knew what I had to do. I changed into my swimming trunks, snuck around the side of the house, grabbed the hose and destroyed her with water. She didn't stand a chance. That is…until it was her turn and she blasted me with her bucket of water. We both laughed and yelled as an all-out battle ensued. This back and forth only lasted about five minutes before I was down for the count, but it's a memory she will carry with her.

Your "yes" and your "no" are designed for relationship. I believe that is why God tells us "no" so often. I imagine He uses a similar (but far more effective scale) when we ask for things. His scale often seems to be the answer to this question: "Does this bring my son/daughter closer to me?" I have found that His "yes" and His "no" tend to focus on drawing me nearer to Himself. If that is our Father's scale, it should be ours as well.

If you're co-parenting, be mindful of your motives. It's easy for your "yes" to stem from competition rather than genuine love for your child. But here's the truth: both of you can be the fun parent. You don't have to outshine each other. You just have to show up with love. Motives matter.

And this isn't just a co-parenting trap—married couples can fall into it too. When one parent feels like the disciplinarian while the other gets to be the "fun one," resentment can build. Parenting isn't a competition; it's a partnership. A strong, united front is one of the best gifts you can give your child.

If this sounds exhausting, you're right. Intentional parenting is exhausting. But it is when we use our responses intentionally with the purpose of relationship that they gain value. Do you want your child to trust you? Be intentional with your answers. If they have experienced that your responses are focused on shepherding their heart, they too will begin to focus on the relationship rather than your answer.

Most generations pick one word (yes or no) and latch on to it, and generations tend to alternate. Children of a "no" generation tend to compensate by making sure that their kids are never without. They become a "yes" generation. Children of a "yes" generation tend to be less sacrificial and more entitled, which leads them to say "no" to their kids more often. This is a dramatic oversimplification of the process and yet, we need to break the cycle. The problem is that none of us have perfect parents, which should be a relief because you aren't going to be the perfect parent either. And yet, we have a Father who is perfect. If we are to break generational patterns and tendencies, we need to press into a deeper relationship with the Dad that dads harder than the best of us.

The key? Intentionality. Let your "yes" and your "no" be grounded in purpose. The win is that you can put parameters around it to help guide you and make this intentional decision a little easier. Here are some questions that I ask myself before giving a response.

1. Does it help grow our relationship? If we are to disciple our kids well, we need to have a strong relationship and fellowship with them. We need to be intentional about developing deep trust and taking opportunities as they come.

2. Why am I saying no? Sometimes it's because we're tired or don't want to get up. We need to measure whose heart we are caring for with our "no". You still need to have ways to prioritize yourself, but sacrificial love should be the pattern.

3. Why am I saying yes? We have a rule in our house. We do not negotiate with terrorists. Just kidding, but really. We don't. Our daughter knows that if she throws a tantrum, the answer locks in as a "no." Throwing a fit cannot become a manipulation tool for our kids. This one is tough because you will pay the price when you begin to put it into practice. IMPORTANT: There is a difference between throwing a fit and being sad. It is okay to be sad, but it is not okay to be rude.

4. What are you afraid of? It's amazing how easily the perceptions of other parents can drive our own behaviors. It's easy to believe that your child's struggle is a reflection upon you, which leads us to want to appease them while in public. I get it. This is a real tension for me as well. Remember, it is not about what other people think, it's about shepherding your child's heart.

Here is the beauty: when we give intentional answers, our "yes" and "no" gain value! It shows our children that we aren't bent toward their desires or our own. Rather, it shows that we have their hearts in mind; it tells them that we can be trusted.

Sometimes the hard thing is the most loving thing. Sometimes saying "no" is a beautiful expression of sacrificial love. Sometimes "yes" says "I choose you over myself". Sometimes the risk of now is worth the rewards of later. Being the primary discipler of your kids is a HUGE task. These tools will not make it easier. I'm serious. In fact, I guarantee that living this out will be more taxing on you (especially at first). Jesus never promised that discipleship would be easy. He did the opposite. He tells us that the road ahead will be difficult and full of trials. That is the path of a disciple, and that is the path of parents who refuse to compromise in their decision to disciple their kids (Matt. 8:18-22, Acts 9:16). It won't be easy —but it won't always be a difficult, uphill struggle. So often, we as Christians think if it's not hard, it's not God. That isn't true. He has good plans for you and your kids. Parenting is hard, but it's also good. It's vulnerable conversations by the fire and laughter around the table. It's making 'tired' wait so you can give one more piggyback ride. It's years from now, watching your kids baptize their kids and standing in awe of how much God has lavished His love upon you. Sure, it'll be difficult, but few things are more meaningful, more lasting, or more worth it.

Reflection

1. When your child asks why, how do you tend to respond?
a. Would your child consider you a safe place to ask questions? If you're not sure, ask them!
b. What happens inside of you when your child asks a question that you don't have the answer to? Do you puff up, self-protect, deflect the question, secretly find the answer yourself or invite your kids to join you?

2. On a scale from one to ten, how are you at celebrating your family?
a. What are some things that your kids are doing right now that you want repeated?
b. What's stopping you from putting this book down right now and celebrating these wins?

3. Are you quick to react or do you take a healthy response time?
a. What "protocols" can you set in place to slow your reaction time a little? Prayer, taking some intentional time, and asking curious questions are excellent ways to help yourself respond well.

4. Do you tend to say "yes" or "no" more often? Why is that?
a. How can you be more intentional with your answers?

Challenge

Say "yes" to the next relational invitation that your child gives you and say yes loudly! It could be playing catch, playing dolls, riding a bike, or going to a movie. This isn't the time to drag your heels to display that you are being sacrificial. Be a joyful sacrifice! Whatever it is that you do, let your yes drive you closer in relationship.

Control or Direct

Our family was invited to a beach house in Galveston to celebrate my buddy Keith's birthday. We arrived at the beach house, ready to celebrate, and Keith told us he had just one birthday wish. He wanted to set off fireworks by the water. We headed to the garage to grab the supplies we thought we'd need for the night ahead. Here's some advice about fireworks—don't try to control them. Don't try to dictate how high they explode, the colors they emit, or how fast they fly. To control fireworks, you'd have to surrender to them. Trust me, your fingers will thank you.

Our kids are just like fireworks. They're meant to be brilliant displays, captivating those around them and pointing the world to look up. But as parents, we often cling to control. And sometimes, our reasons for doing so seem valid. We don't want them to fail. We want to shield them from the same mistakes we made growing up. We think we know best (and often, we do), so we strive for our own version of sovereignty. Yet, when you hold on too tightly to the firework, don't be shocked when it blows up in your face.

Your kids were never meant to be controlled. That's why it often feels like the tighter your grip, the harder they push back. The truth is, parenting isn't about control for two very important reasons:

1. God doesn't control. He sets captives free.
2. Eventually, they will have control of their lives.

If control were God's priority, the story of creation would look very different. But the truth is, God isn't in the business of control. He desires free worshippers who choose Him willingly. His glory shines brightest through our freedom. Imagine how the first chapters of Genesis might have unfolded if God's goal had been control instead of choice.

1. There would have been a "no snakes" policy in the garden.
2. The tree of knowledge of good and evil would not have had fruit or been in the garden at all.
3. He may have put an electric fence around the tree.
4. Before Eve decided to take a bite, He would have jumped out of the bushes and yelled, "Surprise!"
5. Parseltongue would not have been a thing (for you Harry Potter fans).
6. Man would not have had the ability to disobey God.
7. Man would not have been able to believe lies.
8. Man could have been created deaf, blind, and without taste (all of which were used to entice Adam and Eve into their poor decision making).
9. God could have gone full on helicopter parent and never let them be alone.
10. God could have given Adam leadership courses.

God isn't interested in control; He has chosen love instead. True love can only exist within the context of freedom. It must be a choice. That's precisely why God allowed the means of our fall to stand at the center of the garden.

> **True love can only exist within the context of freedom.**

Your children were created as powerful, wonderful beings with the potential to light up the darkness. Yet in our fear, we often hinder them by trying to control what they become. But again, I say: you don't control fireworks—you direct them.

Now, don't mishear me: freedom is not the absence of boundaries. Giving your child choices isn't about losing authority. It's about building responsibility.

We're talking about creating a space where our kids can make choices, which takes us back to the garden!

God gave Adam and Eve a place to worship, work the land, and rule. Were there things beyond Eden? Of course! Just look around. We're living there. But the garden was the boundary God provided, a space where they were free to make choices. One such freedom was the opportunity for man to name the animals. We once gave our daughter a similar privilege in our house, which is why our cat's name is Emmy Unicorn.

While reading Danny Silk's book *Loving Your Kids on Purpose*, one idea struck me profoundly: I can either tell my kids what the right choices are or teach them how to make those choices for themselves. The first option is about control; the second is about direction.

Your child is powerful, and they should know it! The wick is already lit, and they are headed somewhere. When we try to control, we risk slowing their growth and creating resistance as they push against our grip.

Here's the question: what's the difference between a firework and a missile? A firework is directed upward, designed to inspire awe and wonder. A missile, on the other hand, is tightly controlled and devastating to everything nearby.

When we fight for control, we lose the ability to guide. Most parents don't control their kids because they want to hinder them. We all want our children to win and thrive, but the truth is, we don't always know how.

As a pastor, I've met many students who have turned into missiles. They've fought so hard against the control imposed on them that they no longer care where they're headed or who they might hurt. All they know is that they want to be free. Let me be clear: the solution isn't the removal of all guardrails or granting absolute freedom. Kids aren't ready for that kind of responsibility. I'm certainly not handing my five-year-old a box of firecrackers and a lighter, expecting her to make good, wise decisions. This is where intentional discipleship becomes critical. Our kids need guides, someone to walk alongside them as they stumble forward. Guiding and directing our children is a role we must take seriously because if we don't, someone else will.

The fireworks we bought for Keith's birthday were amazing. Among our supplies, we even found metal guides designed to hold the rockets, ensuring they launched straight into the sky. As we lit up the night, we eventually stumbled upon a rocket that was larger than all the others. This one was the grand finale!

Excited, we brought out the rocket, only to realize it was too big for the guide we had. Sure, there was a larger guide back at the house, but that felt miles away. So, we did what any responsible adults would do. We moved a hundred feet down the beach, balanced the rocket precariously on top of the guide (genius, right), and whispered a quick prayer. I then sprinted back to our group of friends, scooped up my daughter, and positioned her securely in my arms behind our not-military-grade golf cart. Yes, I know—I'm absolutely nailing the dad game. Meanwhile, Keith and another friend scanned the area like they were on a covert mission, lit the rocket, and bolted like two middle schoolers ditching detention.

And then... nothing.

I kid you not—nothing happened for what felt like an eternity. I remember thinking, *Well, that's anticlimactic. Guess it's a dud.*

And then, everything happened at once.

First, the rocket ignited. But since it wasn't properly secured to the guide, it had tipped over and decided to embrace its new destiny as a horizontally-launched missile. This thing wasn't aiming for the sky. It was in full-on ground assault mode.

Second—and I swear I'm not making this up—an SUV appeared out of nowhere, cruising down the beach at precisely the wrong moment. It was as if the universe had set the stage for maximum damage.

What happened next felt like slow motion. The missile, now a renegade firework of doom, launched straight toward the SUV. As it hurtled over the hood, it detonated in a dazzling explosion. It must have been the most beautiful and terrifying thing the driver had ever seen. So the police officer driving the SUV (yes, this really happened) turned on his lights to let us know that we were in big trouble. And that, my friends, is why I'm writing this book from prison. Just kidding! But for a moment, I was absolutely convinced we'd be explaining ourselves to a judge. There was no way this officer would believe it was an accident, not with a firework-turned-missile exploding over his hood.

I handed our daughter to one of our friends, took a deep breath, and started walking toward my two very guilty-looking buddies. In that moment, I made a decision. If they were going to jail, I wasn't letting them go alone.

But then, something unexpected happened. The officer turned off his lights and kept driving down the beach. The lesson here? Fireworks aren't meant to be controlled, but they do need to be directed by a proper guide. Without it, the consequences can be explosive—literally and figuratively.

You are meant to be the guide. Your child was uniquely designed for you to shepherd their heart with intention and love. If we don't take on that role, we're leaving a void, inviting someone or something else to step in and lead them instead. You are their primary discipler. Own it.

> **You are their primary discipler. Own it.**

Consider this: a study by Lehigh University found that 70% of criminals come from broken homes (households where the roles of parents have been fractured, divided, or even abandoned altogether). As for the remaining 30%, many likely grew up in homes that appeared stable on the surface but lacked intentional guidance and leadership.[3]

Getting rid of boundaries isn't the answer. Kids crave structure and leadership, which is exactly what parenting is designed to provide. We're their guides, here to inspire them to reach new heights. But if you try to control them, expect resistance. Our job is to set up enough guardrails to keep them safe while giving them room to take risks, make choices, and, yes, sometimes fail—preferably without requiring stitches. It sounds simple, but in practice, it's a delicate dance—one that requires just as much learning for us as it does for them.

Most families have one parent who leans toward control and another who's more of a "Go ahead and climb that tree—only one way to find out if that branch can hold you" type. Neither approach is completely right or wrong. But if you can both move toward the middle, this concept starts to click. It's not about control; it's about providing direction. So what does that actually look like? Let's talk about it.

Don't Tell Me What to Do

I enjoy troubleshooting and problem-solving. It's encouraging when people seek my help, and I'm eager to provide immediate and clear solutions whenever I can. While there's nothing wrong with offering assistance, I must be cautious not to make it about giving answers (driven by my pride) instead of empowering others to find their own solutions. The first approach creates a dependency on me, while the latter means I'm essentially working myself out of a job. Perhaps you've heard it said this way. "Give a man a fish, and you'll feed him for a day. Teach a man to fish, and you'll feed him for a lifetime." This is what healthy direction looks like.

Jesus had this unique approach that He used often—it's like a Jedi mind trick. You can't read a Gospel without seeing Him use it a dozen times. Here's how it worked. Someone would approach Jesus with a question, and His response would

---

[3] Raymond Bell et al., *The Nature and Prevalence of Learning Deficiencies among Adult Inmates* (Bethlehem, PA: Lehigh University, 1983), [page number if applicable].

often be another question. He gave them space to wrestle through the answer. We often see the experts of the law, the Pharisees, and even His disciples grappling with the questions Jesus posed, struggling to find the right answer.

Here's the key. Jesus wasn't asking for advice because He didn't know the answer. He had been teaching in the temple since He was a boy and had the deepest possible relationship with the Father. He is God. Jesus knew the answers, but He was deeply invested in teaching His disciples how to fish for answers themselves.

This is a valuable discipleship practice for all ages. When our kids bring us their questions, we give them space to contribute to the answer, and we do this for several important reasons.

1. It helps them learn where to find answers.
2. It encourages them to think critically themselves.
3. It helps provide direction without controlling.
4. Their answers will give you clear insight on where they are spiritually.

That fourth reason is crucial. As disciple-makers, we need to understand where our children are in order to help them take their next step toward maturity. When they offer their own solutions, we gain a clearer picture of their current thinking. Some questions you can ask to guide this process include: What do you think? If you were in my position, what would you say? Can you think of anything in Scripture that might speak to this?

If we're in the business of directing, we can't leave it to just asking questions. It would be irresponsible to ask our kids for their thoughts and then send them on their way. Their answers may be spot on, or they might be a bit off. This is where we dig deeper by asking more questions to get to the heart of the issue. If possible, it's helpful to hit the pause button and say something like, "Let's pray about this for the week. As you wrestle through it, I want you to dive into God's Word and see what it says. Then, next week (set a specific time), we'll talk about what we've learned." Follow-through is key. They've trusted you and sought your guidance. Don't leave them casting nets on the wrong side of the boat. When you meet again, let them share what they've learned first, and see how it aligns with what you've discovered.

And just like that, you're guiding your child, which is far more important than simply giving an answer. You've just taught them where to find the answers, and even though you're a valuable source of wisdom, you're showing them how to interpret God's Word—something far, far better.

If you're reading these words and feeling overwhelmed—maybe you're a single parent, living in a divided home, or just plain tired—I see you. I'm not preaching from a mountaintop. I'm right there with you in the valley. Parenting is exhausting, even before you add intentionality to the mix. Start small. Be intentional at dinner this week, or set aside a specific time to ask your kids good questions. It's less about getting it perfect every time (which often fuels our desire to control) and more about taking a step-by-step journey toward maturing our kids by giving them direction and then letting them run.

Give Choices

One of the most challenging aspects of being young is the sense of powerlessness. I remember struggling with that feeling during a season of my life when I longed for more than I was being given. I didn't know Jesus, and I certainly didn't know how to process that feeling, but I remember grappling with the sense that I was completely at the mercy of others. Kids are accustomed to having rules imposed on them and are expected to follow them, often without understanding why those rules matter. But what happens when they are suddenly granted complete freedom?

A study by Lifeway Research found that about 66% of high school graduates drift away from their faith to some extent.[4] Having finally tasted freedom,

---

[4] Aaron Earls, "Most Teenagers Drop Out of Church When They Become Young Adults," *Lifeway Research*, January 15, 2019, https://research.lifeway.com/2019/01/15/most-teenagers-drop-out-of-church-as-young-adults/.

these young adults move away from what they were told to do and begin making decisions for themselves. But what if we approached this differently? What if we allowed them to make choices from the start and intentionally reminded them of their power? I'm not suggesting we give them complete control. If I put my five-year-old in the driver's seat and asked her to take us somewhere, chances are high that we'll crash (if she can even reach the accelerator). As I pay to repair our car and garage door, I'll wonder why I trusted a five-year-old with a motor vehicle. This isn't about handing over the reins to our children. Rather, it's about creating opportunities for them to make decisions while you act as a safety net. We can tell our kids what the right choices are, or we can teach them how to make the right choices for themselves. The first is like a lecture-style course, while the latter is what Jesus did as He walked alongside His people.

> **We can tell our kids what the right choices are, or we can teach them how to make the right choices for themselves.**

This process has brought me so much freedom in my own parenting. Crazy, right? I give up some control and gain freedom in return. What's even crazier is that our kids will feel the same way. Our daughter has two main areas of the house that are primarily hers: her bedroom and the loft. While she does a good job keeping the mess in check, if we wait long enough, both spaces will eventually need a good cleaning. At that point, I could simply go to her and say, "Alright, sweetheart, clean your room, and once you're done, clean the loft." I'm well within my authority to expect her to clean her spaces. Not only that, but it's also important for her to learn to take care of her things. But I'd like to suggest an alternative approach. Rather than telling her what to do, I try to give her the choice. I've found that it's more effective to say, "Hey sweetheart, I noticed the loft and your bedroom are a little messy. What do you think about that?" There's a clear answer here, and she's smart enough to figure it out—both spaces need cleaning! Once she identifies the need, I offer her another choice: "Would you rather clean the loft or your room first?" The task still gets done, and I'm instilling accountability and responsibility in her, but I'm also giving her the power to decide some of the steps. When my connection with her is strong, giving her the choice is exactly what she needs to feel excited about starting the task. She has control, and I'm simply a guide.

Admittedly, your child might not see the point. You give them a choice, but they remain unmotivated and uninterested. They'd much rather watch TV than decide between doing the dishes or folding laundry. Or maybe they actually *prefer* paper plates and don't mind their clothes in a heap on the floor—so to them, both options seem pointless.

That's okay! This is exactly what you've been preparing for. You've trained your whole parenting life for this moment. Don't rise up in frustration. Stay level. Remember, your kids don't have the authority or maturity to control you—so don't let them. Instead, patiently walk them through the *why*. The *why* gives the *what* its value, and sometimes, their resistance is just a lack of understanding.

Explaining might help. It might not. And if it doesn't, that's okay too—because this is an opportunity for them to practice honoring their parents, even when they don't fully understand. Let them know that throughout life, they'll be asked to do things that seem silly or trivial, but that doesn't make them any less necessary.

As parents, it's easy to push our kids toward simple obedience, but that's not what we should aim for. Obedience for obedience's sake is meaningless. In Matthew 15:9, Jesus addresses this directly: "They worship me in vain; their teachings are merely human rules." To God, the answer was never more rules, which is why His Gospel isn't based on fear. Jesus didn't walk around holding signs telling people to love Him or go to hell. While He did discuss hell, it was never meant to invoke fear. Love casts out fear. It doesn't embrace it. One of God's most common phrases in Scripture is "Do not be afraid." His goal was always for us to fall in love with Him. We can do all the things—obey His law, perform miracles, or witness to thousands—but if love is absent, so is the value (1 Corinthians 13). Love gives purpose to everything we do.

"Go clean your room, or else! Don't talk back to me, or you'll be grounded for a week!" Many of us heard these phrases growing up, and just as many of us have said ourselves. And every one of them is rooted in fear. We tend to believe that an external, rule-based system can work its way into a child's heart. This model is seen in Scripture. The Israelites were constantly required to follow external rules to be right with God, but the purpose of this system was to show our desperate need for God's grace and mercy. Then, God changed the system through Jesus. Where external governance once ruled, we've now been given the Holy Spirit (internal governance). This Spirit works its way through our souls and into our hearts. God's plan has always been freedom, not control. That's why, as we are transformed from the inside out, we begin to bear fruit on the outside.

This inside-out system is built on love and leads us to freedom. We have the power to choose. Does that mean all choices are good? Absolutely not. But when my goal is God's heart, that will often guide me to make the right choices.

Why do you obey God? Is it out of fear of hell or eternal punishment? Or is it because you love Him? If your answer is fear, let's pause for a moment. I challenge you to open your Bible to the Gospel of John. As you read, pay attention to how Jesus interacts with those around Him. Is it fear that draws people like Philip and Nathanael, Nicodemus, the woman at the well, Mary and Martha, and others to Him? Love is meant to be the driving force as we press forward toward the goal. As a parent, I'm modeling an outdated system when I use fear tactics (intentionally or unintentionally). We need to recognize that love, not fear, is meant to govern our actions.

I remember a time when Jennie was taking a nap, and I knew the house needed cleaning, so I started doing the dishes. It had to be done, and since I was the only one awake, I figured it had to be me. As I worked, I noticed my frustration growing with Jennie. Why? Had she demanded I do it? Had she been rude or unkind? No. I was angry because I was the one doing the work. It's amazing how easily I can revert to a child in an adult's body. There have been other times when I did more than just dishes—entire days spent cleaning the house. I'd have worship music blasting, feeling excited for Jennie to come home and walk into a house so clean she could eat off the floor. The only difference in those two situations was my motivation. In one, I felt obligated by external circumstances; in the other, I was motivated by my love for her.

Our kids shouldn't be ruled by external factors. Consequences are real but shouldn't be the primary reason our kids obey. I want my daughter to make the right choices because she loves me, her mom, her brother, and especially Jesus.

As parents, we have the opportunity to allow our kids to make choices and learn from them. In *The Divine Mentor*, Dr. Wayne Cordeiro explains that there are two ways to choose correctly: wisdom or consequence.[5] With wisdom, you heed the counsel of others; with consequence, you learn the hard way. If you haven't figured it out by now, I'm the type who tends to choose the second option. Often, it's my own fear that prevents me from letting my family learn that way as well. I'm not saying consequence is the preferred method, but how else can someone learn that wisdom is the better option? Probably by experiencing that consequences are worse. The truth is, when given choices, we all make mistakes. I'd much rather my kids mess up while they're still at home, with Jennie and me there to catch them on the way down.

Stop Fighting for Your Kid

For a while, our daughter had a drinking problem. More specifically, a "drink problem." Wherever she went, her water bottle seemed to stay behind. I can't tell you how many times I'd get her buckled into her car seat, start the car, and then hear from the back, "Dad, you forgot my water." "No, tiny human, you forgot your water." It constantly drove me a little crazy, so I devised a plan.

One Saturday morning, we picked up donuts and brought them home for breakfast. It was a beautiful day, so as a family, we went into our backyard to soak it all in. As we sat down, I heard it again. "Dad, you forgot my water." I took a deep

[5] Wayne Cordeiro, *The Divine Mentor: Growing Your Faith as You Sit at the Feet of the Savior* (Minneapolis, MN: Bethany House, 2007), 30.

breath and replied as gently as I could, "I'm really sorry you don't have your water, honey. What are you going to do about it?" She looked at me and politely asked, "Will you go get it for me, please?" Okay, this is what we train for… "No, honey, I won't." A wave of relief washed over me as I realized this wasn't my fight. I didn't need to solve every problem my child faced. She's brilliant! I fully believed she was capable of solving this on her own. She didn't need me to fight for her; she needed me to remind her that she had the power to find a solution.

Parenting is tough, and this is a hard lesson. We see our child struggling, and naturally, we want to help because we love them. Your desire to help isn't wrong, but sometimes the response is. When I do everything for my daughter, I teach her that she's the center of the universe, that she's dependent, and that she doesn't have the strength to solve problems on her own. Is that my intention? No, but it's the message that gets communicated.

I'm not saying that when your child struggles to swim, you should let them go under. What I am saying is that as your child grows, they become more capable and should become less dependent. If you slow down and give them space to find their own solutions, you'll be amazed at what your kids can come up with. When in doubt, start small. After all, I'm just talking about a water bottle.

As soon as I told Lilla that I wasn't going to help, she lost it. Our backyard has an iron fence, so the neighbors didn't need to buy tickets to see the show. It was truly something special, and my role in it was to simply be love. I wasn't choosing not to help my daughter because I didn't love her. I was doing it because I do. I want her to grow into an independent, godly woman who understands how strong she truly is.

At this point, Lilla was beside herself. She went from crying to anger, then back to crying with anger. Here's the thing: my plan didn't involve making her feel alone or abandoned, but I did want her to put in the effort. So, I asked if she wanted help making a plan. She looked up and answered with one word: "Yes."

"Well, baby, I have a couple of options. You could go inside and fill up a cup." She was frustrated. This was exactly what she didn't want to do. "I'm not done," I replied. "You could drink out of the dog bowl." Admittedly, it would have been pretty gross, but I was committed if that's how she wanted to solve her dilemma. Her face told me she'd prefer another option. "Or you could drink from the hose." Her eyes lit up. "I can drink from the hose?" "You bet," I said. "How do I turn it on?" I showed her where the nozzle was, and she figured it out from there. Like I said, she's brilliant! By the end, she was fully hydrated, completely soaked, and proud of herself. She had worked to solve her problem. She didn't need Dad or Mom or anyone else. Lilla had the power to solve her water bottle problem.

It's easy to continuously see your child as the baby they once were. As parents, we naturally want to be needed and helpful, so we often jump at every opportunity. The challenge, though, is that as our kids grow, they'll need less help—and that's a good thing. We must learn to give them room to grow and help them understand their own strength. It's time to stop fighting their battles for them and start training them to fight for themselves. The goal in raising godly men and women is that they won't need you, but they'll still want you around.

In John 6, Jesus speaks a hard truth. We won't dive into the details, but it involves eating His flesh and drinking His blood. Yes, you heard me right. This is why it's important to read your Bible! There's some wild stuff in there. Jesus shares this truth, and many of His disciples are taken aback, questioning how they could possibly believe what He was saying. At this point, most pastors would start to get nervous. They'd notice the crowd thinning out and scramble to find ways to keep people around. "We need better music! We need a softer message!" But not Jesus. He kept speaking the truth, and as a result, many left Him (it's even titled that way in Scripture). When He looked around, only twelve disciples remained. This is the "free t-shirt" phase of ministry. "Oh, you stuck around? Alright, get these guys some shirts." But don't worry, He wasn't going to soften His message. He wasn't about to stop speaking truth, even if it was hard.

Jesus wasn't trying to shield people from the truth. He wanted them to fight for themselves, so He pressed in. "You don't want to leave too?" He asked, giving them an out. If they stayed, they had to know why. There had to be more to their commitment than Jesus protecting them or making His truth easy to swallow. Because, in the world's eyes, the truth is rarely easy to accept, and for the disciples, most would eventually die for their faith. Jesus gave them the choice, and Peter responded, "Lord, to whom shall we go? You have the words of eternal life. We have come to believe and to know that you are the Holy One of God" (John 6:68-69).

Jesus essentially asks, "Why on earth would you stay?" and Peter replies, "How could we ever leave?! We know too much; we've seen too much!" Jesus didn't shield them from the truth. He gave them the ability to choose well—and they did.

You won't always be there to fight their battles for them. You won't share a dorm room or navigate hard conversations with professors. You won't go on dates and argue with their significant other (at least you shouldn't). If you don't prepare them along the way to advocate for themselves, they'll become co-dependent adults who don't know how.

So, out of love, here's a hard truth: *You are not the hero of your child's story.* You won't be there for every problem or every heartbreak. No amount of security can shield them from life's difficulties. The best thing you can do is train your child for battle and prepare their heart. Stop fighting for them. They have more strength than we often give them credit for.

Discipline

When it comes to discipline, we have a choice. Yet, for generations, one option has been embraced far too easily: passivity. When a problem arises, we can choose to let it slide, to turn a blind eye. In the moment, it feels easier—but passivity isn't neutral; it's a decision in itself. Intentional love is never passive. Yes, it gives our kids space to make mistakes, but it also holds the line and points them toward something better. Passive parents drift with the current; intentional parents push against it. That's why discipline isn't just necessary—it's an act of love. And it starts with a plan you're committed to holding firm.

That doesn't mean grace gets left out. If you want to raise disciples, steady doses of grace are essential. The key is intentionality. When your child makes a mistake or poor choice, you need to prayerfully discern whether grace or consequences will best serve them. Here's a hint: if the behavior is recurring, grace alone isn't the answer. They need to learn that real choices carry real consequences. But there will be moments when your child expects you to drop the hammer—and instead, you take them out for ice cream. They already know they messed up. This is your chance to remind them that their mistakes will never outrun your love. And don't worry, you can grab a cookie dough Blizzard for yourself, too.

When it comes to discipline, allowing our kids to choose has been a game-changer in how we approach discipline. To be honest, I struggled for a long time with how to discipline our daughter, especially since Jennie and I often leaned in opposite directions. I tend to be stricter when it comes to enforcing expectations and believed that spanking, when done appropriately, was acceptable. Jennie, on the other hand, leaned toward more leniency and wasn't at all on board with spanking. This book won't delve into the spanking debate. The key point is this: discipline was an area of disunity in our marriage, and we had to come together in prayer to find unity and a shared approach.

In my experience leading other parents, this topic is one of the most divisive. As I worked through where our family stood, I decided to try something new: giving my daughter choices in her consequences. Rather than saying, "This toy is a problem, and you're losing it," I try to focus on her heart and offer a choice. For example, I might say, "Hey sweetie, I notice that your toys are leading you to act a bit mean. Which one would you prefer to lose for now: your stuffed unicorn or the bunny?" It might sound silly, but as I've integrated this into our discipline, I've seen our daughter feel empowered, knowing she still has some control.

But be careful! Our kids are incredibly smart, and they can tell when we aren't serious. Don't bluff. I'll say it again—don't bluff! If you give them a choice and they make one, you must follow through with their chosen consequence. If you don't, you're undermining the progress you've made. For example, what happens if five minutes later, I come back because she's crying, and I give her back her stuffed unicorn to placate her? I've just taught her two things: you can't trust my word, and your feelings are in charge. Without realizing it, we teach our kids that their emotions—especially their volume—can control us. The purpose of offering choices is to give our kids freedom so they can learn to control their own actions, not so they can control us. Never offer an option you're not willing to follow through on. This is the most common place where parents undermine their own authority.

Whether you're married or co-parenting, this is an area where you need a unified front. Kids cannot learn that they can play one parent against the other. They can't believe that if one parent enforces consequences, they can run to the other to receive a manipulated grace.

In our house, we have a simple rule: *Jennie and I are a team.* That means what Mom says, Dad says—and vice versa. Seeking a second opinion from the other parent isn't just undermining authority; it's considered dishonest in our home because the answer has already been given (not by one parent but by both). Do Jennie and I always agree? Of course not. But as a team, we handle those disagreements behind closed doors. We might huddle up, talk it through, and decide to take a different approach—but that conversation doesn't happen in front of young ears and is never in response to them choosing to undermine a teammate. Our kids need to see that Mom and Dad stand united. And that level of parental unity can still apply as you co-parent. Don't argue or undermine the other parent when you pick up or drop off your kid(s). Don't do it openly over the phone. Schedule a time to have a conversation where you both can come to an agreement. Just because you live in different places doesn't mean you can't co-parent as a team.

The toughest part of discipline for me has always been guarding my own heart. I want to get mad, angry, and throw my own adult version of a tantrum, but I am powerful enough to control my response.

When I was in the Army, we spent significant time training. We learned how to wear our uniforms, salute properly, clean and use our weapons, and practice basic combat strategy. We didn't do this for fun or because we wanted to. We did it because a battle was ahead, and we needed to be prepared. As parents, it's easy for us to rush into the battle unprepared, without the right training, equipment, or strategy. We can't continue like this. There is a very real enemy out there (Satan), but we tend to see the battle and, because we're untrained, fire at the nearest person. This is how friendly fire happens. We often hit the wrong person in conflict, mistaking them for the enemy. God designed your family to be on your team to advance His Kingdom, yet the enemy would love nothing more than to convince you that your spouse, child, or someone else is the problem. We easily fall into the lie that they are the enemy. But the truth is, there is an enemy, and his main goal is to make us forget which team we are on.

It's the worst feeling in the world when I mess this up as a parent, when I let the switch in my heart flip, forgetting that my child is another tiny team member I'm meant to walk beside and love. They aren't the enemy. Do they make mistakes? Do they cause hurt through immaturity? You better believe it. But when your teammate is confused about their role on the team, you don't attack them. You coach them, train them, and equip them to rally forward toward the goal.

I can easily forget this if I'm not guarding my heart and leaning on Jesus. I need to put on the full armor of God so that I'm not convinced my child, who is using their power to turn the bedroom into a disaster zone, is the enemy. Armor up, parents! Train up! This is a battle, and your child doesn't yet know how to wield the weapons they have. You may get hurt a little. But don't forget, they've always been and will always be on your team (even if they forget).

The irony is that when I'm wearing the armor of God, it helps me approach my daughter with vulnerability and honesty. What if, instead of getting angry when our kids lie, we shared how it affects our hearts? "Sweetie, you have my heart, and when you made that comment, it hurt me. I didn't feel loved, and I felt like I wasn't on your team." Don't say this if you're not being sincere. The goal is teaching your kids to care for others, not to give them a lesson in emotional manipulation.

"Josh, that's a great concept, but I'm worried I'm telling my child they can hurt me. I'm telling them they have power over me." Yes and no. Yes, you're giving your child a real picture of relationships and how healthy, love-filled relationships require two actively engaged people. You're absolutely showing them that their choices can either make you proud or cause you pain. And no. Your child does not control you. You are armored up and ready for battle. You know exactly what you're doing, and you're so prayed up it feels like Jesus is holding you steady. You're demonstrating strength and power by showing that, despite your hurt, you are still in control.

I was disciplining a young man who had been getting into a lot of trouble. He'd been kicked out of a couple of schools, and I had even visited him in jail. One day, I asked him why he got into so many fights. He said it was because people kept coming at him, and he wanted them to know who was in charge. I asked him who he thought was in charge, and he smiled and said it was him. I looked him straight in the eyes, which was a risk with him, and said, "I think you're wrong. If I walked up to you right now, karate-chopped you in the throat, and you decided to fight me, who's in charge?" He thought for a moment, then shrugged and said, "I am."

I countered, "No, I am. I decided before I came up to you that I wanted to fight. I asserted my ninja skills over you, and now you're doing exactly what I told you to do." He paused and asked, "If fighting doesn't give me control, what does?" I loved his question. It told me he was taking this seriously. I asked him if he'd ever been rude to me, and he nodded. Then I asked if he'd ever threatened me or wanted to fight me. He nodded again. Finally, I asked if he'd ever gotten a rise out of me. He looked me in the eyes and said, "No, never." I leaned in and said, "You want to know why? I love you, dude. I want you to win. But you will never have that kind of power over me. Are there reasons that might lead me to fight someone? Yes, absolutely. I know exactly what those reasons are, and I've decided them in advance. But no matter what you say to me or try to do, I'm not going to react because if I did, you wouldn't be sitting here with me. I love you, bud, but I am in charge of me. That's what true control looks like."

During this same conversation, this young man placed his faith in Jesus. Was it because I'm awesome? Nope. I simply showed him what real power looks like. He had felt the relentless pull of the current, been dragged into countless conflicts, and struggled for control as he was carried downstream. But in our conversation, he saw that the Holy Spirit's power far outweighed any external force. That was the kind of power he wanted a piece of.

This stuff is so much easier outside of the home. The people we are closest to have the greatest ability to get under our skin, push all the right buttons, and send us over the edge. There have been countless times when I've done the exact opposite in my own home. Once the toothpaste is out of the bottle, it can't go back in, and those moments stick with me, reminding me of what happens when I go in unprepared and without my armor. It's sad, but true: the people we love the most are often the ones we hurt the most. I'm deeply grateful for my wife's strength to endure my weaknesses. Walking closely with Jesus is my best chance to stay armored up and protected while remaining humble and vulnerable. Every moment of discipline is meant to reflect love; turning missiles into fireworks.

Reflection

1. Do you gravitate towards controlling or being more passive with your child?
a. In what areas are you quicker to cling to control?
b. Are there areas where your lack of guardrails has enabled unhealthy behaviors?
c. How has your child responded to your approach?

2. Do you tend to give answers or ask questions?
a. List some go-to questions you can keep ready for the next time your child needs help.

3. What would it look like for you to focus on equipping your child to solve their own problems?
a. What are some common struggles they face and how can you empower them to work toward a solution?

4. Does your discipline focus on an external governing system (rules) or an internal governing system (the Holy Spirit)?
a. How can you shift the "why" away from the rule and toward relationship?
b. What is your part in modeling this new expectation?

Challenge

Where do you struggle most with control in your parenting? Have a conversation with your spouse to strategically identify ways you can focus on guiding rather than controlling. Do you need to give your child more choices, space, or the freedom to experience the consequences of their actions? Whatever your plan, take action now and watch your child grow.

Needs Based Parenting

We can agree that discipleship, parenting, and coaching were never meant to center around the person providing the aid. We never want our desires or abilities to hinder the support we are supposed to offer. And yet, this is the current that parenting often falls into. Is that our true intention? No, but the current seldom aligns with our heart. Raising godly men and women is a dynamic, ever-changing process. Just when you find a rhythm, you're thrown a curveball, and suddenly your role has shifted. The challenge arises when we reach those parenting "sweet spots" where we're thriving, and hesitate to move on. Often, we don't even realize we need to.

Imagine calling a doctor to fix a broken leg, only for her to arrive and start discussing how she'd like to perform heart surgery, because that's her area of expertise. Or picture a home repairman you called, who, instead of fixing your leaky roof, advises you on adding new outlets in your kitchen. What about a missions organization arriving in a third-world country, eager and ready to paint a school, when the actual need is financial support so that children can have transportation to attend the school in the first place (but that's a whole other book). The point is this:

The need should always define the aid. Recognizing the difference between a perceived need and a real one is important. A person addicted to heroin may feel they need money for survival or another fix to ease the pain, when in reality,

> **Our desires and abilities should never dictate the aid and support we offer.**

what they truly need is healing and recovery. The actual need is always what we are meant to support.

At times, our abilities can guide us in determining where to provide support and aid. The point, however, isn't to ignore your abilities, resources, or passions. Most of the time, these are assets meant to be shared with others. But parenting doesn't offer that same luxury. If your parenting approach centers around a "sweet spot" with 5-6 year-olds (because, let's be honest, they're awesome), you're left with limited options. You can either continue treating your teenager like a five-year-old, which is a recipe for rebellion, confusion, and division, or you can "trade in" your older child for a newer model. Obviously, neither is an appropriate option. But the point remains: how we parent must be based on the needs of our children, not our desire for comfort.

In previous chapters, we discussed the importance of knowing where our kids are, so we can help them take the next step. This isn't a destination; it's a continuous pattern. Identify where they are, help them grow, and then check in again to keep leading them forward. The process is ongoing and requires great flexibility from the parent, as you're constantly troubleshooting based on your child's needs, not your own abilities. As soon as you hit a parental sweet spot, prepare for a change.

The problem arises when we fail to establish proper guardrails in our lives, allowing our parenting to become our identity. The irony is that once this happens, our ability to let our children's needs dictate the support we offer becomes limited. If your identity is wrapped up in being needed by your kids, what happens when they no longer need you? Remember, their independence is a key goal of parenting. If your identity's foundation is about being liked by them, it could prevent you from having the difficult conversations necessary for discipleship. But when your identity is rooted in Jesus, change becomes an old friend you've been expecting. You're ready to have those hard conversations, and you hope that, eventually, your children will no longer need you.

I suggest that our roles shift at different stages throughout our children's development, and the more aware we are of these changes, the better equipped we'll be to support their continued growth. If we don't adjust our role to meet their needs, we risk stunting their growth and damaging the relationship. The age ranges provided are merely suggestions and will vary depending on your child's maturity, needs, abilities, and experiences. The goal is not to make you feel guilty if your child falls outside the typical age range, nor to stir unhealthy pride if they exceed expectations. In 1 Corinthians 3:6-9, Paul reminds us that while we have a role to play, God ultimately brings the growth. When we take on more responsibility than we should, we risk trying to take His place.

> **You control the process, not the results.**

Simply put, growth is beyond your control, though you are responsible for your part, God does the heavy lifting. Note that these phases do not have rigid boundaries; each role is meant to gradually merge into the next (which is why the age ranges overlap).

Teachers (0-8 years old)

We need food at every stage of life, but there are few ages where we wouldn't survive without being fed. If you placed a cheeseburger in front of your infant right now, nothing good would come of it. They might turn it into the world's worst version of Play-Doh, but it won't be food to them. They're not ready for it, and they can't feed themselves. Here's the thing about Jesus: He doesn't expect them to. He had a unique way of seeing people and understanding where they were, which helped Him know what they needed to grow. A spiritual infant doesn't need a cheeseburger; they need someone to walk beside them and help them eat. When a crowd surrounded Jesus, He often taught them. He shared truth using parables about parties, farming, and shepherds (topics they would understand). He intentionally met people where they were so they could be fed.

For clarity, let's define "teacher" so we're all on the same page. A teacher communicates truth in a way that allows listeners to learn, be fed, and (with God's help) grow. In simpler terms, it's the mindset of: *I do, you watch.*

In this role, listeners aren't active participants. They are recipients of the teaching. This is usually the easiest stage for us to step into. Teaching (or feeding) is simple and can be done on various topics, especially those the teacher feels comfortable or passionate about. But this also presents a problem.

In discipleship, it's crucial that I take my role as a disciple seriously because we tend to talk about what we're doing well and avoid confronting the areas where we're failing. If I'm not serving within my community, I won't challenge those I lead to serve. Similarly, if I'm not actively tithing and living generously, I won't challenge others to do the same. We rarely inspect areas in the hearts of others that we're not willing to have inspected in our own.

Parents, this is your call to get discipled. Mere church attendance isn't enough, and it's not the example Jesus set for us. I have a responsibility, not only for my own walk but also to truly understand what it means to live out my faith in every area. I mess this up often, but I'm grateful for the people in my life who are willing to walk through those failures with me, allowing even my missteps to be used for good.

Did you know that illiteracy is often cross-generational? When parents are illiterate, their children's literacy levels are directly affected because parents who can't read struggle to teach their children how to read and often can't convey the importance of reading. Unfortunately, we have too many parents who are Biblically illiterate. They rely on a pastor or preacher to guide them each Sunday but don't have the ability to measure what they hear against God's Word. They move forward, blindly trusting the person speaking, hoping that this individual knows God's Word and can interpret it accurately for them. Let me be clear: it's good to have a pastor and church you trust, but if you can't take what you hear and compare it to God's Word, your blind trust becomes a serious risk for both you and your family. In my current city, many people present themselves as pastors but offer flawed and loose interpretations of Scripture. If you don't know God's Word, you risk following a false teacher, and your family is likely to follow you.

In John 10, Jesus speaks of the Good Shepherd. He says the Shepherd's sheep will follow Him, because they recognize his voice. They follow Him because they know Him and would never follow a stranger. They don't recognize the stranger's voice. The Bible is a tool for you to understand who God is and what He desires. You don't need to blindly trust a pastor on stage or someone who happened to write a book. Yes, you heard me correctly—don't blindly trust me. Our responsibility is to measure what we hear against God's Word, ensuring that it aligns with His voice. I'm not saying you need to become a Bible scholar or attend seminary. What I am saying is that we must take our role as family leaders seriously. We are responsible for growing our ability to identify the Shepherd's voice.

And when you hear Him, echo the Shepherd. Echo the Shepherd. Echo the Shepherd. What does it look like to teach your child?

They'll begin to recognize His voice more clearly as you share His truth with them. We cannot move forward Biblically illiterate. You cannot afford to blindly trust that you're following the right voice. Go to the Word of God and measure everything against it. Some people in your life would love to walk beside you and help you along the way.

Echo the Shepherd! As you hear His voice, share it with your family.

At a certain age, my child will no longer want me to turn a spoonful of food into an airplane. They won't want me to feed them by hand anymore (although I may still need to cook). In fact, there comes an age when this will frustrate them, and they might even say, "Stop it, I'm not a baby anymore!" In my experience, as soon as I get comfortable in a role, it begins to change. This doesn't mean you'll stop teaching your kids. On the contrary, we're never supposed to stop teaching. However, the way we lead will change over time.

Facilitators (3-18 years old)

Although teaching is an essential part of the discipleship process, our children were never meant to remain in that stage. If we settle here, we foster a consumer mindset, which has become a cultural norm in America, which teaches that discipleship is the church's responsibility, not the design of your home. While your church and community are meant to equip and empower you as you lead your family, they are poor substitutes for the disciple-maker you've been called to be. Too many churches focus on filling seats and emphasizing the Sunday experience, neglecting their members' roles as shepherds. When we attend solely for the experience, we forget we're meant to be partners, driving toward the destination together. If we only teach, we miss the next step in growth and, in turn, hinder that growth.

Early on, our role as teacher begins to shift. You are no longer just a teacher; you become a facilitator. Let's define that. A facilitator invites those they lead to engage with and participate in the truth they are learning. They don't send their disciples off on their own yet and are often still present to assist, but the facilitator actively works to involve those they lead in applying what they've learned and then debriefing how it was applied.

Teacher: I do, you watch.
Facilitator: I do, you help. You do, I help.

At this stage, a shift in ownership occurs. The young disciple is no longer completely dependent on their parent but is now being equipped and prepared to become a disciple and eventually a disciple-maker.

Jesus was constantly creating opportunities for His disciples to learn and apply the truths they had received. In Luke 10, He sends His disciples to the towns He would later visit. He sent them out in pairs and gave them specific instructions on what to bring and how to act when they entered a home. Jesus could have easily done all of this Himself, and truthfully, He would have done it better. But He didn't do it for them. Instead, He entrusted the responsibility to His disciples, allowing them to learn, grow, and apply what they had been taught. I imagine this left the disciples feeling empowered, as though they had a meaningful role in the ministry. The more we involve people, the more ownership they take in the process. We want our kids to be fully committed to Jesus, and that means providing them with opportunities to actively engage in the process.

In our student ministry, we've cultivated an incredible worship experience. Our team creates a Holy Spirit-led environment, intentionally crafted, and full of shepherding opportunities. There have been several instances where I've followed up with team members to tell them how something they shared deeply impacted me. Here's the amazing part: our team is student-led, except for one person. The students have been invited to take ownership of their role in the ministry, actively leading and shepherding from the stage. This doesn't happen by accident. When I first came to our church, our team was comprised of paid musicians. But over time, our leaders intentionally invited students into the process and gave them opportunities to contribute. We are actively empowering these students while showing every other student that they too can make a difference! And the beauty of it is that it's not just about music. We've had students deliver messages and return as interns. Our tech team is entirely run by students, except for our tech director, who was a student we eventually hired as staff! We are intentionally giving away responsibility, and it's creating buy-in and driving spiritual growth.

Parents, we aren't just called to be teachers. Early on, we are meant to become facilitators. We are called to give pieces of responsibility to our kids, allowing them to begin owning their faith. For example, when Lilla receives birthday money, I ask her how much she wants to give back to God. I want her to get excited about the opportunity to give back to God what is already His, and to understand that money isn't the real goal. I'm giving her the chance to practice the truths she's been taught. Do you have a family devotional? Let your child lead it! Will they nail it? Maybe, maybe not. But that's okay because facilitation is about more than just delegation.

Yes, a facilitator gives pieces of responsibility away, but they also create a space to return, debrief, and reset. Jesus didn't just send His disciples out in pairs. He had them come back and report what they experienced. As they did, they shared how incredible it was, even mentioning that demons were submitting to them in Jesus' name. This was exciting news, but Jesus wasn't finished. He reminded them to rejoice not in the power they had been given, but in the fact that their names were written in Heaven (Luke 10:17-20). It was time to debrief everything that had happened, and Jesus used this opportunity to shepherd their hearts.

If we only give pieces of responsibility away and never discuss what happened afterward, we miss a vital shepherding opportunity. In many ways, we're setting them up to fail. Our student worship team debriefs after every session. They talk about how they led specific songs, transitions, and teaching moments, discussing what went well and identifying areas for growth. Without debriefing, we leave room for our kids to make the same mistakes repeatedly, without them being aware of the error or possibility for improvement. The worst part is that these issues could be blind spots for them, blind spots that won't be addressed until someone loves them enough to have the difficult conversation.

As we lead our kids as facilitators, we actively provide them with opportunities to engage and then come together to discuss the experience. During this time, our kids can take ownership of their faith, use their passions for Kingdom impact, and draw others closer to Jesus. It will be a powerful season of growth that will mature both child and parent, helping them both become more like Jesus.

Coach (15 - 25 years old)

Up until this point, things are going fairly well. The distinction between teacher and facilitator is clear and essential for a child's growth. However, a shift occurs during our kids' teenage years—one that many parents struggle to accept. As our kids grow, they naturally seek more freedom, while parents cling desperately to control. Why do we do this? Is it because we don't love them, or because we don't want them to succeed without us? No. From my conversations with parents, it's evident that the majority of us are simply afraid. We raise our children to be godly men and women, yet releasing them to stand on their own feels like a risk we're reluctant to take.

Every May, we host a graduation dinner to celebrate sending our students—these disciples—out into college, work, or discovery. We celebrate our belief that these students will defy the statistics and remain faithful. At every graduation dinner, I give the same speech. I tell parents that, whether they like it or not, their role has shifted. It's no longer just about teaching or facilitating—they are now coaches. I challenge parents to ensure their home becomes a place their kids want to return to.

> **Coaches don't run the plays. They guide from the sidelines.**

A coach's role is to create a safe, welcoming environment that their disciple can come back to regularly. The disciple has been sent out and actively engages in God's mission, but they often return to their coach for guidance, wisdom, and fellowship.

At this stage, your job is no longer to make decisions for them but to provide perspective, wisdom, and encouragement as they navigate life's challenges.

Teacher: I do, you watch.
Facilitator: I do, you help. You do, I help.
Coach: You do, I watch.

Here's the problem: We struggle when our kids no longer need us. We often wonder what we're doing wrong when they no longer want our help. It's easy to feel unwanted or unimportant, which leads us to question our identity as their parent. This sets off an all-too-common cycle: The child pulls away. The parent holds tighter. The child pulls away. The parent grips harder. The child pulls away. The parent grits their teeth, determined to hold on for dear life (and we wonder why we have so much back pain as we get older). If we paused for a moment, we'd realize that the child pulling away isn't a child anymore. This young man or woman has been prepared for this moment. They are ready and eager to grow, succeed, and even fail, all while learning to stand on their own.

The crazy part is that our struggle with this is misguided because this is exactly what winning looks like. We're meant to make disciples who are eventually sent out. Sending them is part of their growth. I'm not suggesting we should be overjoyed at the thought of our kids leaving our home. As a parent, I'm not looking forward to any of them leaving. I'm not thinking about it. I'm not ready. Please, don't do this to me…

It's okay to mourn a little, as the relationship shifts. But you need to understand that the more you hold on, the more they'll pull away. The cost of this relational tug-of-war is your fellowship. It sends the message to your child that they can't come near you because you won't let go. There will come a point when your child is ready and needs to be sent. While bittersweet, don't lose sight of the victory in that moment.

Your role as a parent isn't over—it's just different. As a coach, you must create a safe space for your child to come for counsel and biblical wisdom. But a safe space doesn't mean telling them only what they want to hear. There were many conversations I didn't want to hear, but my parents knew I needed when I was in my early twenties. If they hadn't shared those hard truths with me, I may not have woken up to my desperate need for Jesus. A safe environment involves these three things: being available, being honest, and maintaining a strong embrace with a loose grip.

Quick reminder: Your advice should be invited. As a coach, you have to be okay with your kids—who are no longer kids—running their own plays, taking risks, and learning from their hits. Your young adult needs both a space to play and the freedom to fail. Your job is to be accessible, not invasive. There will be times when you clearly see the right choice—but you also know they're going to make their own decisions anyway. Instead of inserting yourself into moments where they need to learn by experience, focus on being a safe place for them to land when things don't go as they hoped. Be available and approachable. No one wants to hear, "I told you so." Use discernment to recognize when something is truly worth speaking up about and when it's an opportunity for them to grow on their own.

Paul and Timothy provide a powerful example of this stage. Timothy had been released by Paul to disciple others and was entrusted with leading other church leaders. Paul didn't hover over Timothy or constantly hold his hand. No, he sent him out to do the Lord's work. Was Paul an absent father? Not at all. He simply provided the freedom for Timothy to be sent and become who God intended him to be. Even in that freedom, Paul still checked in, offering encouragement, challenge, and development for Timothy's ministry.

"That's easy to say. That wasn't Paul's kid."

Well, Paul did refer to Timothy as his spiritual son multiple times, but fair point. James and John were two brothers who loved to fish with their dad. Fishing wasn't just a hobby; it was their livelihood. One day, a teacher named Jesus came along and asked them to follow Him. This wasn't a casual invitation, like "Follow me down the block for dinner." No, it was more like, "I'm about to change your life. You'll follow me in such an extreme way that it will cost me my life—and many others will follow me to the same fate." In this story, we don't see Zebedee, their father, protest when his sons decide to follow Jesus. We don't see him complain about how much harder it will be to provide for his family with two of his workers gone. There's no evidence that Zebedee tried to stop them at all. They were called, it was time, so he let them go.

However, parents should still be involved, and their role is not only recommended but essential—just in a different way. A coach doesn't run the plays during a football game. In fact, in most sports, a coach isn't even allowed on the field. The coach's primary responsibility is to communicate the strategies, guide the players, and then debrief and equip them after the game. Your young disciple is about to face all kinds of challenges they've never encountered before—relationships, cultural opposition, and doubts they'll have to confront. If you try to jump onto the field and run the plays for them, a flag will be thrown, and a penalty assessed. Players want to play. They're eager to take what the coach has taught and apply it. Personally, I've always found it amusing to watch spectators jump on the field and start running around. During this week's Monday Night Football game, a man ran onto the field, apparently for a gender reveal. Bobby Wagner, a future Hall of Fame linebacker, stepped through the pink smoke and swiftly flattened the guy. He crumpled beneath the force of a man who's built like a cement truck. He'll likely make a great girl dad (once he recovers enough to walk again). Players don't appreciate it when the wrong people step onto the field. That's no longer your role. Do so at your own risk. Instead, you might occasionally be invited into the huddle between plays or into the locker room after the game. Here, you can provide a space for your player to debrief, learn, and grow.

Of all the role changes, this one is the most noticeable. You're no longer holding your child's hand as they cross the street; instead, you answer the phone when they call. This stage offers a wonderful opportunity for growth, and you will continue to see the fruit as long as you maintain a strong, supportive relationship with your child. During times like these, it's important to remember that your goal in parenting was never to raise a godly boy or girl who depends on their parents. As we disciple our children intentionally, we're raising godly men and women who seek out their parents for wisdom. Part of growing up is leaving home, but how tightly we hold on often determines whether they're running away or being sent. The former brings relational turmoil; the latter, celebration.

Co-laborer (Ages 26-Facetime with Jesus)

Each stage brings its own victories, but it is this stage toward which all the others lead. This is the *iron sharpens iron stage*. Here, you may find you are learning just as much from your child as they are from you! This is an extraordinary time, offering us as parents a moment to check our pride and remember that we, too, must remain coachable.

A co-laborer is someone who is equipped and ready to do the work. They might still need guidance and support, but they are cultivating their own harvest and are responsible for mentoring others. In other words, they are mature, intentional disciple-makers who approach their role with seriousness and purpose.

Teacher: I do, you watch
Facilitator: I do, you help. You do, I help.
Coach: You do, I watch.
Co-Laborer: You do, with someone else.

Unfortunately, reaching this phase has become increasingly rare. The only way we can get there is by taking our role of intentionally discipling our children seriously. And there are two key reasons for this.

The first reason is that our kids need to be invested in profoundly over many years (even decades) so they can mature into the disciples God created them to be. My grandpa is a master gardener. Papa takes immense pride in the plants he nurtures, and he loves giving tours of his garden, showcasing the meticulous care he takes to ensure each plant gets exactly what it needs. He has bananas, tomatoes, and countless other plants that I couldn't identify without his help. Even though there are dozens of varieties in his care, he knows exactly what each plant requires. He understands the right amount of water, the type of sunlight needed, and the optimal planting time. To reach this phase with our kids, we must know them in the same way. This may seem intimidating, but as you've learned in the previous chapters, you're not doing it alone. Watching our kids grow to become co-laborers is a monumental victory for both parents and children.

The second reason reaching this stage is uncommon is that parents must also prioritize their own growth. You can only lead someone to the place where you are; you can only give what you've received. If your growth stalls, you'll either limit their growth, or they'll eventually outpace you. I'm not saying they will leave you, but they may stop depending on you in certain areas. A wise person seeks counsel from someone who is deeply rooted in God and has experience in the subject. I wouldn't go to a serial dater for marriage advice, ask someone struggling with anger for guidance on managing rage, or seek parenting advice from someone who doesn't have children. It simply wouldn't be wise. Parents must continually find ways to prioritize their own growth in Jesus, or risk being outpaced by their kids. To be clear, we don't pursue Jesus merely to prevent our kids from "outgrowing" us. But if I truly love God, I can't help but press into a deeper relationship with Him—and in doing so, I am transformed. Even though it's a win when our kids mature, Jesus desires our hearts too.

In Scripture, we see Paul and Peter as prime examples of co-laborers. Both men were extraordinary leaders, leaving lasting impacts on the foundation of God's church. These were capable leaders who could have functioned independently, but instead, they chose to unite. They gathered to check in, debrief, celebrate, and, at times, for a healthy rebuking (Galatians 2). Though they didn't share the same children—Peter focused on the Jews, while Paul ministered to the Gentiles—they still partnered together as co-laborers, often from a distance.

What a victory it is for parents who have reached this stage! Most of us will spend our lives working toward this goal. If we take our role seriously, pray fervently, and rely fully on God, we may one day look across the field and witness our children harvesting their own crops. Pursue this goal with determination, and remember: every challenge is an opportunity to draw closer to this beautiful destination.

Reflection

1. Based on your child's maturity, which role do you need to step into more fully?

a. If you have multiple kids, identify the different roles that your children may need you to function within.
b. Have you been functioning in the correct role?
c. What is the relational cost of operating in the incorrect role with your children?
d. If you are in the wrong role, what are you risking or sacrificing by stepping into the correct one?

2. How can you prepare for the next role that you will take on?

Challenge

Identify the role you are meant to fulfill, and if married, discuss it with your spouse. Write down two ways you are currently fulfilling that role, as well as two areas where you can improve. Then, hold each other accountable in working toward those goals. If you have a healthy co-parenting relationship, this exercise could be beneficial as you work together to raise your child(ren).

Don't forget—it takes a village to raise a parent. No matter what stage you're in, seek wisdom from those ahead of you and learn from their experiences. Ask yourself: Who in my life is a step ahead? What insights can I gain from them? At the same time, look to those in an earlier stage. How can you support and encourage them as they navigate the path you've already walked? Parenting isn't meant to be done alone—it's a journey best traveled together.

Own It

I've been sitting in this coffee shop for a while now, searching for the right words to conclude this journey—a journey as profound as guiding our families toward a path that defies the norms of this world. A small book, penned by an admittedly inexperienced author, might seem insufficient to equip anyone for the challenges ahead. Yet, I believe these are words you need to hear.

You are exactly where you need to be. That's it—you're doing it! Whether this book has validated your discipling strategies from the past few years or you're standing at the starting line, desperate to reach your teenager's heart, you are exactly where you need to be.

To be clear, this isn't a call to stay where you are. A still target is an easy target. But there is victory in reaching this point—right here, right now—a turning point. My prayer is that you won't let the journey end here. Too many books are read and conferences attended, leaving us inspired for change, only to be swept back into the current weeks later. Don't let this book be just a moment. Let it spark a generational movement that flows from you to your children and through theirs beyond. You are exactly where you need to be, and yet, we all must forge upriver toward the Source.

If there are two takeaways from this book that I hope you hold on to, they are these: Be present and be intentional. Use your time with God, your spouse, and your child as an opportunity to invest in the Kingdom for His glory. It won't be without challenges—mistakes will happen—but this rising generation cannot afford for passivity to shape their lives. As intentional parents, we must take a stand for our families and strategically push back against the current. This requires a deliberate mental shift.

Joshua addressed this concept as he led the Israelites into the land of promise.

He declared: "But if serving the LORD seems undesirable to you, then choose for yourselves this day whom you will serve, whether the gods your ancestors served beyond the Euphrates, or the gods of the Amorites, in whose land you are living. But as for me and my household, we will serve the LORD" (Joshua 24:15).

Scripture doesn't tell us who Joshua's wife was or how many children he had, but it does tell us this: Joshua took ownership of his family's path. He refused to let passivity or the world's current dictate their direction. Instead, he boldly declared to everyone who would listen: This is where we are going, and we are getting there together.

That's what this book is—a declaration of war against the current that has been pushing parents around since humanity's fall from the garden. It's an unequivocal rejection of passivity and a lack of intentionality that leaves our families vulnerable and unprepared for the spiritual battles they will face. If ever there was a time to start discipling your kids, that time is now.

Just yesterday, I was sitting in a child dedication class at our church when I heard someone declare that if we disciple our kids, it guarantees they will grow up knowing Jesus. Oh, how I wish that were true. As a parent, I wish I could have that much control.

This person wasn't making an egregious theological leap. They simply misunderstood the purpose of a passage from Scripture. We've referenced this passage in earlier chapters, but it's crucial to provide clarity here. Proverbs 22:6 says. *"Start children off on the way they should go, and even when they are old they will not turn from it."* Here's what we need to understand: context matters. This passage comes from the book of Proverbs, which, as the first seven verses make clear, aims to impart wisdom. These are principles, not promises.

That's an important distinction. If this verse were a promise, it would be a surefire guarantee that you could control your child's eternal destination. And who wouldn't want that? Parenting would feel far less terrifying if we had that kind of power. But remember, God's pursuit isn't about control. He desires free worshippers, which means that, ultimately, your child will have to make their own choice. Proverbs 22:6 is not a promise. It's wisdom imparted as a principle from the wisest man to ever live (apart from Jesus).

Here's what I mean. Jennie's previous job was to help people who were blind regain their independence. She equipped them to navigate their homes, cross streets, and get to work. One client, in particular, still stands out in her mind.

Jennie was teaching a young woman how to cross a busy highway. As always, she began by asking the client to demonstrate how she would typically cross the street. The idea was to establish a baseline. The client hesitated and asked, "Are you sure?" Jennie assured her and stood back to observe. What followed left Jennie both terrified and amazed. Her client raised her long cane in the air, shouted, "Living on the edge!" and darted into the highway.

After recovering from the anxiety of nearly losing her client, Jennie firmly told her, "You can never do that again." Then, my wife taught her how to cross the street properly, and they spent time practicing together. Here's the principle: if you learn to cross the street the right way, you're more likely to live longer. Visionless Frogger is not a recipe for good health. But is that a promise? No. Her client could still be struck by lightning, no matter how carefully she crossed. However, by following Jennie's wisdom, her chances of a long life significantly increased.

Just because this passage isn't a promise doesn't mean it lacks value. The principle matters! Show your kids the way they should go, and they'll have a much better chance of developing their own, personal relationship with Jesus. But at the end of the day, it's their relationship which means it will ultimately be their choice.

Every relationship has three parts: my part, their part, and God's part. The challenge is resisting the current's pull that can drag you into a function that isn't your own. God will always do His part. He nails it every time. But I can only control my own. I can't do my kid's part for them.

This should bring freedom, not chains. A limited role is a gift because you are a limited being. You aren't meant to take on God's role under your own power. Rather, you are meant to do your part under God's power. He is the one who gives you the strength and endurance to be present and intentional. He is the one who helps you do your part.

Trying to do more than your part only sets you up for failure. Taking on the role of your children leads to rebellion, and taking on God's role *is* rebellion. You are not the hero of your kids' story. It is Jesus who is working to draw near the hearts of your children, just as He has done for you.

> **You get to determine whether He works through you or in spite of you.**

Does that mean you could do your part as an intentional, godly parent and still raise a child who rejects God? Yes. Parenting is scary. But according to Proverbs, our kids are more likely to do their part when we do ours. Ultimately, God will do what God does, but

You cannot save your kids, but you can point them to the only One who ever could.

In the book of Joshua, the man after whom the book is named took a stand and made it clear that he was choosing to intentionally lead his family. My family needs me to lead them. Your family needs you to lead them. Anything less is a poor substitute, and frankly, these weak parental imitators are running the show. Technology, pop culture, endless hours of TV, friend groups, the gods of the Amorites, YouTubers, anything with a following—each would love nothing more than to parent your child for you. They cry out, "Don't worry, we'll take it from here." They want to assume the role that God chose for you (and they wouldn't mind trying to take God's role, too). They take the title, take the role, and lead your family further downstream.

Do not defer the role the Lord has given you. We have a responsibility to guide our families to the feet of Jesus. We must own it, or someone else will. And that brings us back to the point: be present and be intentional. If we do these things, while staying connected to Jesus, we will bear much fruit.

My prayer is that we will continue to march upstream. I pray that we are so caught up in Jesus that He gives us the strength to press forward against the tide. As we push onward, may we lift our heads and see that we are not alone. Who knows, maybe we'll even see each other along the way. If you do, be sure to say "Hi." Together, we can remind the current that it doesn't control the direction of our parenting, that it doesn't own the trajectory of our families—that our households will serve the Lord.

A Parent's Guide to Sharing the Gospel with Kids

Sharing the gospel with your child is one of the most meaningful conversations you can have. This guide will help you explain the Good News of Jesus in a simple, relatable way while leaving room for questions and conversation. Remember, this conversation is rarely a one-time event that happens in 5–10 minutes. It is far more likely that the following steps will play out over many conversations, which may take weeks, months, or years.

Step 1: Prepare Your Heart

Pray First: Ask God for wisdom, the right words, and for your child's heart to be open to receiving the message.

Know the Basics: Be clear about the gospel message yourself. At its core:

- God loves us and created us to know Him.
- Sin separates us from God.
- Jesus lived a perfect life, died for our sins, and rose again to bring us back to God.
- We respond by trusting Jesus and following Him as King and Lord of our lives.

Step 2: Explain the Gospel in Simple Steps

Use kid-friendly language and examples they can relate to:

1. God Loves You and Made You to Be Close to Him

- *"Did you know God made you and loves you more than anyone else ever could? He made everything in the world—like the stars, animals, and you—so we could enjoy life with Him."*
- Use **Genesis 1:27** (*"So God created mankind in his own image..."*).

2. We All Mess Up (Sin) and Can't Fix It on Our Own

- *"Sometimes we do wrong things—like lying, being mean, or disobeying. That's called sin, and it separates us from God."*
- Explain that no one is perfect, and we all need God's help.
- Use **Romans 3:23** (*"For all have sinned and fall short of the glory of God."*).

3. Jesus Came to Fix What's Broken

- *"God loves us so much that He sent His Son, Jesus, to take the punishment for our sins. Jesus died on the cross and came back to life to make a way for us to be close to God again."*
- Use **John 3:16** (*"For God so loved the world that he gave his one and only Son..."*).

4. We Can Say Yes to Jesus

- *"Jesus made a way for us to be close to God, but we have to say yes to His gift. Saying yes means we believe in Jesus, trust Him to forgive our sins, and want to follow Him."*
- Use **Romans 10:9** (*"If you declare with your mouth, 'Jesus is Lord,' and believe in your heart that God raised him from the dead, you will be saved."*).

Step 3: Make it Relatable

Use Stories or Analogies:

- A broken friendship can illustrate how sin separates us from God, and Jesus fixes the friendship.
- A gift analogy: *"Jesus gave us the free gift of forgiveness, but like any gift, we have to choose to accept it."*
- Dirty shoes analogy: *"God is perfect and keeps a clean house. The only problem is that you and I have really muddy shoes. Our shoes are so muddy, that we can't become clean on our own. When we accept what He did, Jesus gives us new clothes (shoes too)!*

That means on our own we couldn't enter the house of God, but with Jesus we can walk in with confidence!"

Ask Questions:

- "What do you think sin is?"
- "Why do you think Jesus died for us?"
- "Does this make sense to you? What questions do you have?"

Be Honest: If your child asks a question you don't know, it's okay to say, *"That's a great question! Let's figure it out together."*

Step 4: Invite a Response

Explain How to Respond to the Gospel:

- **Believe:** Trust that Jesus died for your sins and rose again.
- **Repent:** Turn away from sin, ask God for forgiveness, and seek His help to follow Him daily.
- **Follow:** Ask Jesus to be the King of your life and for Him to teach you what it looks like to live in His Kingdom.

Model a Simple Prayer:

- *"Dear Jesus, I know I've done wrong things. Thank You for dying for my sins and coming back to life. I trust You and want to follow You. Please forgive me and help me live for You. Amen."*

Be Patient: Don't pressure them. Some kids may respond immediately, while others may need more time.

Step 5: Help Them Grow

Celebrate Their Decision: If they say yes to Jesus, celebrate with them and affirm how proud you are of their decision.

Encourage Next Steps:

- Read the Bible together, starting with stories about Jesus (e.g., the Gospels).
- Pray together daily, showing them how to talk to God.
- Get them involved in church and age-appropriate discipleship activities.

Tips for Sharing the Gospel

1. Be Genuine: Kids respond to authenticity. Share your own story of faith in a way they can understand.

2. Use Age-Appropriate Language: Keep it simple and relatable for their level of understanding.

3. Answer with Grace: Be ready for questions or doubts and respond with patience.

Major Themes of the Bible

As parents, one of the most important things we can do is teach our kids about God's story—the story of who He is, what He has done, and what that means for us. But sometimes, knowing where to start can feel overwhelming.

This resource is designed to help. These major themes of the Bible provide a simple, clear guide to the foundational truths that shape our faith. As your kids grow, these themes will help them understand the big picture of God's love, His rescue plan through Jesus, and His invitation for us to be part of His mission.

Use this as a tool for conversations, bedtime discussions, family devotions, or everyday moments when big questions come up. Our prayer is that it helps you confidently disciple your children, leading them to know, love, and follow Jesus with their whole hearts.

1. God Made Everything (Creation): A long time ago, before anything existed, God made the world and everything in it—stars, animals, plants, and even you! He made everything good because He loves us (Genesis 1:1-31).

2. We Messed Up (Sin): God gave people the freedom to make choices, but the first people, Adam and Eve, made a bad one—they disobeyed God. That's called sin, and it separates us from God (Genesis 3:1-24).

3. God Has a Plan (Promises): Even though we messed up, God promised to fix everything. He chose people like Abraham, Moses, and David to help show His love and plan for the world (Genesis 12:1-3, Exodus 3:10, 2 Samuel 7:12-16).

4. God Sent Jesus (Rescue): To fix the problem of sin, God sent His Son, Jesus, to save us. Jesus taught us how to love God and others, died on the cross for our sins, and came back to life to show His power over sin and death (John 3:16, Luke 24:1-7).

5. We Can Be Close to God (Salvation): When we trust in Jesus, God forgives our sins, and we can be part of His family forever! This means we get to be close to God, just like He wanted from the beginning (Ephesians 2:8-9).

6. God Gave Us a Job (Mission): Jesus told His followers to share His love and good news with everyone in the world. That's why we love others, serve people, and tell them about Jesus (Matthew 28:19-20).

7. God is Always With Us (Holy Spirit): After Jesus went back to heaven, He sent the Holy Spirit to help us. The Holy Spirit lives in us, gives us power to follow Jesus, and helps us make good choices (John 14:26, Acts 1:8).

8. God is Fixing Everything (New Creation): One day, God will make everything perfect again—no more sadness, sickness, or sin. We will live with Him forever in a new and beautiful world (Revelation 21:1-4).

A Sample Sabbath Schedule for Families

Why Sabbath Matters for Families

Sabbath is a gift from God to help us rest, worship, and love others. It's a time to pause and remember that God is in control. By observing a Sabbath, your family can grow closer to God and each other while learning to trust Him in all things.

What is Sabbath?

Sabbath is a day blessed by God and set aside for rest and worship. One of the most important rhythms in the life of Jesus was stopping to rest and delight in God's presence. Yet in a world that constantly pulls at our attention and fills our schedules, rest feels nearly impossible, especially for young families. Between work, school, activities, and endless to-do lists, slowing down can seem like a luxury we can't afford. But Sabbath isn't just a day off—it's a gift from God, designed to refresh our souls and reorient our lives around what matters most.

For many, practicing Sabbath is new, and the thought of setting aside 24 hours might feel intimidating. But the goal isn't perfection. It's presence. Start simple: choose a 24-hour period to rest and worship. Mark the beginning and end with a small family ritual—lighting a candle, saying a prayer, sharing a meal together. Then, fill the day with things that bring joy and refreshment—good food, outdoor walks, unhurried conversations, worship, laughter, and moments of stillness.

It may feel countercultural (and even a little chaotic at first), but Sabbath is one of the most life-giving practices for families today. So be patient with yourself, your kids, and the practice itself. As you embrace Sabbath, may you find the "rest for your souls" that Jesus so graciously offers.

- **Morning:** Enjoy a family breakfast and read a Bible story.
- **Midday:** Go for a walk or play outside.
- **Afternoon:** Do a quiet craft, read a book, or rest.
- **Evening:** Share a simple dinner, talk about the day, and thank God together.

Sample Schedule of What The Nation Family Sabbath Looks Like

Here's an example of how our family celebrates Sabbath that is filled with rest, worship, and time together. While Thursday evening to Friday evening works best for our family, you choose the best day for yours. If you find it's a struggle to find any time that works for everyone, it might be an indication that priorities need to shift.

1. Thursday Afternoon - Prep for Sabbath:

- Clean the house, do the dishes, and prepare dinner and meals for Friday.

2. Unplug:

- Put away phones and computers. As much as possible, avoid work and digital devices.

3. Thursday Evening - Begin Sabbath:

- Share a family dinner, talk about the week, and what you hope God will do during your Sabbath rest.
- Take a family walk around the neighborhood.
- After putting the kids to bed, relax with a glass of wine and read or talk on the back porch.

4. Friday Morning:

- Spend time with Jesus in the morning with a good cup of coffee (or your favorite morning beverage).
- Enjoy a family breakfast (homemade waffles are our favorite!).

5. Rest and Worship Throughout the Day:
Do whatever feels restful or worshipful for the family. Some examples include:

- Stream worship music on the TV and have spontaneous dance parties with the kids to their favorite worship songs.
- Take family walks.
- Play in the pool.
- Draw, color, or paint.
- Build something creative with wood.
- Enjoy delicious food prepared the day before.
- Have a workout, go for a run, or bike ride (if exercise feels restful and energizing for you).

Enjoy your Sabbath—it's God's gift to you!

Acknowledgments

First, I want to thank my bride, Jennie. Honestly, she deserves an entire book of acknowledgements—one so big it would make Goliath nervous. A single paragraph could never capture the depth of my gratitude for her. Jennie, thank you for pushing me to risk for the Gospel, for being my teammate in everything, and for always being the love of my life—even when I make you mad.

Matt Nations has profoundly impacted my life, and he's earned his place here long before this book ever had words. With all the time, reading, feedback, writing and endless re-rereading, Matt's contribution deserves to be written in bold from here on out. **In fact, bold it is. Thank you for discipling me and showing me how to be a godly man, husband, and father. I'm honored to co-author this book with you.**

Christy Goldsmith, Stevo Foster, and Chase Reed played a huge role in getting this book off the ground, constantly encouraging me to keep going. John and Shireen Rand, y'all are awesome. Thank you for all the insights that helped us equip families of all dynamics. And Torrie Sorge and the Growmentum Press team helped us bring it all to life. Thank you for taking on our first book and making what we started even better.

A special shout-out to Saulo Nate, an incredible friend who designed the cover of this book. If you need design work, check out Pixel Grove Studio—you won't find better. Fun fact: Saulo actually created his own font, which you can see on the cover. I didn't even know you could do that!

Finally, to our church communities—Riverside Church, CyLife Church, and 180 Life Church. The impact you've had on our family has exceeded all expectations. Thank you for walking alongside a broken guy like me and helping me continue to stumble closer to Jesus.

~ Josh Poteet

First, I want to thank my bride, Jess—your love, wisdom, and encouragement mean more than words can express. Thank you for believing in me, for your unwavering support, and for the way you faithfully walk alongside me in life and ministry. Our family is my greatest joy, and I'm honored to pursue this calling with you.

To my children, Kai, Jayse, River, and Shiloh—you are a constant reminder of God's goodness and grace. My prayer is that you grow to know and love Jesus deeply, and that our home is always a place where discipleship happens in the everyday moments.

To Josh Poteet—thank you for your friendship and inviting me to write this book with you. Your passion for discipleship and leadership is contagious, and I'm grateful to serve alongside you in this mission.

To Riverside Church—thank you for allowing me to serve and lead among such an incredible community of believers. Your commitment to making disciples and building God's church fuels my passion for ministry.

To the team at Growmentum—your dedication to equipping and supporting church leaders is inspiring. I'm honored to work alongside you all as we help churches align vision and strategy to advance the Kingdom.

~ Matt Nations

About the Authors

Joshua Poteet is the Lead Pastor of 180 Life Church in West Hartford, CT. Previously, he served as the Next Gen Pastor at CyLife Church, where he led and developed the leaders of the kids, students, and young adult ministries. He holds a Master's in Theology and has been part of the Relational Discipleship Network for 10 years, leading discipleship trainings, both in the U.S. and internationally.

Josh regularly teaches on equipping parents, empowering disciples, training leaders, and helping families embrace their role as primary disciple-makers. His passion for family discipleship is shaped by his personal experiences as a father and his years of walking alongside parents as they raise up tiny disciples.

He and his wife, Jennie, live in Connecticut with their two children, Lilla and Ezra.

Matt Nations is the Executive Pastor at Riverside Church in Fort Myers, FL, and a team member at Growmentum Group, where he helps churches align vision, strategy, and structure for greater kingdom impact. With years of experience in church leadership, pastoral coaching, and organizational development, Matt is passionate about helping churches create intentional pathways for spiritual growth and mission-driven effectiveness. He has had the opportunity to lead discipleship training for many churches in the U.S. and around the world.

Matt's heart for discipleship and leadership development is shaped by his own ministry journey and his commitment to seeing people grow in their faith and calling. He and his wife, Jess, live in Florida with their four children, Kai, Jayse, River, and Shiloh.

Thank You for Reading!

If you've made it this far, we just want to say—thank you. We hope *Parenting Against the Current* has been helpful, encouraging, and a clear call to disciple your kids with intentionality and grace.

If you enjoyed the book, we'd be incredibly grateful if you took a moment to leave a review. Whether it's a few lines or a detailed reflection, your words help other parents discover the book and start their own journey upstream.

Scan the QR code below to leave a review on Amazon—or share your thoughts on Goodreads, Fable, or wherever you found the book. Every review helps the message reach more families.

Thanks again for reading!

Josh & Matt

Stay in Touch

We're so glad you joined us on this journey.

If this book encouraged you, raised new questions, or sparked meaningful conversations in your home—we'd love to hear about it. Your stories matter to us.

Whether you're looking for more resources, want to share how God is moving in your family, or just want to say hello, we'd be honored to connect.

We're also available to speak at conferences, camps, churches, and other gatherings where families and leaders are being equipped to disciple the next generation. If that's something you're planning, we'd love to be part of it.

You can reach us here:
Email: **ParentingAgainstTheCurrent@gmail.com**
Social Media: **@ParentingAgainstTheCurrent**

We're cheering you on as you continue to parent with purpose and push upstream. You're not alone.

— Josh and Matt

www.ingramcontent.com/pod-product-compliance
Lightning Source LLC
Chambersburg PA
CBHW071213090426
42736CB00014B/2804